CHUCK GARRISON'S
OFFSHORE FISHING
SOUTHERN CALIFORNIA AND BAJA

Chronicle Books / San Francisco

This book is dedicated to my Uncle Phil, who first taught me a love for fishing and who so baited my interest that it led to a career of writing about the outdoors.

I greatly appreciate the contribution of Jack Samson, editor of *Field & Stream*, in preparing the Foreword to this book. I also wish to thank Al Tetzlaff for the use of his photographs of striped marlin, and extend my thanks to Karen Green and Betty Black for their saltwater fish recipes.

Special thanks are due my wife Cindy, who struggled with a malfunctioning typewriter in preparing the final draft of the manuscript.

CHUCK GARRISON

Library of Congress Cataloging in Publication Data

Garrison, Chuck.
  Offshore fishing in southern California and
Baja.

  Edition of 1977 published under title: Offshore
fishing in southern California.
  1. Saltwater fishing — California, Southern.
2.   Saltwater fishing — Mexico — Baja California.
I. Title.
SH473.G37 1981   799.1'6   80-27579
ISBN 0-87701-166-4

Contents

Foreword

I am always flattered when asked to do a foreword for a young outdoor writer's book. Perhaps it is because, in spite of a lifetime of writing about hunting and fishing, it is always a surprise to find out one is considered an expert. In the hunting and fishing field everybody is an expert and the proof is in the landing, tagging or bagging of game.

If the proof of Chuck Garrison's ability is in the catching, then this book has got to be a success. I have fished with Chuck—in his own balliwick, Baja—and if there is anymore enthusiastic or proficient salt water big game angler than Garrison I have yet to meet him.

Chuck grew up working the partyboat circuit of Southern California and the waters off Baja. He learned the tackle and terminology while a youngster and later refined the techniques of catching everything from yellowfin tuna to blue marlin while an outdoor writer. He fishes with a flair.

If there is any one sign that a man will be great, and not just a good fisherman, it is the sheer enthusiasm with which he faces each new day on the water and his attitude when losing fish. To Chuck Garrison there is no such thing as a bad fishing day and a good fish lost simply means a wait until another one strikes. He is a happy man around other fishermen and is one of that rare breed of young people today: a dedicated outdoorsman.

Jack Samson
Editor
Field & Stream

Owners of private boats make up a very high percentage of Southland offshore fishermen. This center-console-model craft sports such features as a bow-mounted fighting chair, fish-storage boxes, cutting board, rod racks, outrigger poles, and collapsible foul-weather canvas coverings.

Introduction

Modern ocean sportfishing along the Southern California coast puts to shame the crude angling practices of the late 1800s. *Sport* fishing then was unheard of; those who did battle with hook and line were not yet regulated by a code of ethics that promoted a sporting contest. Off Catalina Island, for instance, heavy handlines were used and giant bluefin tuna were often landed in no more than five minutes. Usually the disposal of such a grand fish was equally disdainful: The catch was fed to the sharks.

In 1898 things began to change. Repelled by the practice of handlining, Charles F. Holder organized the Tuna Club of Santa Catalina Island, the world's first organization of deepsea sportfishermen. Holder said of the group:

> The public supposed it was a fishing or angling club to catch tunas, but the original institution which I drafted with Mr. W. H. Landers read: The Tuna Club of Santa Catalina Island, California, is hereby formed. . . . The object of this club is the protection of the game fishes . . . to encourage and foster the catching of all fishes, and especially tuna, yellowtail, [white] seabass, black seabass, etc., with the *lightest rod and reel tackle*, and to discourage handline fishing, as being unsportsmanlike and against the public interest. [italics mine]

According to the California Department of Fish and Game, there were few boats for hire at Avalon before ocean game-fishing became a rod and reel sport, but under the stimulus of the well-to-do Tuna Club membership, boatmen eventually numbered from 50 to 100. Like partyboat operators today, these early boatmen provided their customers transportation, and fishing know-how, and fishing know-where.

The early fishing launches, 18 to 20 feet in length, seated only one or two anglers. Although the craft were built by a local shipyard and were similar in appearance, they ranged in value from $800 to $3500. Boat power increased over the years, from the 8 to 10 horsepower of the first engines, to a grand 40 horsepower by 1912.

In August 1913 an area three miles wide entirely encircling Santa Catalina Island was established by law as a sportfishing reserve. This later proved to be the first move in a controversy—commercial versus sportfishing—still simmering after some 60-plus years.

During those early years of sportfishing in Southland waters, bluefin ("leaping") tuna were the most-sought game fish. Also available were marlin, yellowfin tuna, albacore, giant black sea bass, white sea bass, yellowtail, and such "lesser" fish as barracuda, bass, and bonito.

Offshore tackle began to improve after the establishment of the Tuna Club of Avalon, Santa Catalina Island, an organization formed to promote sportfishing. This early big-game reel is believed to have been custom-made for famous author Zane Grey.

Described by some observers of the time as "the finest sea angling in the world," Southern California ocean fishing produced some enviable catches. The largest bluefin tuna taken on rod and reel—among Tuna Club records—weighed 261 pounds and was caught in 1899. The first light tackle record, set with a 145½-pound tuna, was established in 1919. Other all-tackle records of the period which bear evidence of the fish-rich waters included: marlin, 405 pounds (1932); broadbill swordfish, 573 pounds (1927); black sea bass, 493 pounds (1916); yellowtail, 60½ pounds (1908); white sea bass, 60 pounds (1904); and albacore, 66¼ pounds (1911).

In 1919 alone, a combined total of 911 bluefin and yellowfin tuna was caught at Catalina Island and recorded by the Tuna Club. A full 36 of these weighed over 100 pounds each, and some approached 200 pounds.

Publicity of the early sportfishing catches eventually fostered a rising interest in deepsea angling by the general public. In 1919 there were practically no facilities for ocean sportfishing except skiffs or expensive charter boats, but between 1929 and 1939 a fleet of over 200 partyboats went into operation.

In 1933 G. H. Clark and Richard S. Croaker, of the California Department of Fish and Game, wrote of "live bait" partyboat fishing, and indicated that live bait was in use here at least as early as 1925. These boats were said to have regular daily schedules and accommodated an average of 30 fishermen.

Today the Southland partyboat fleet numbers in the hundreds and contains some of the most modern and luxurious vessels in the country. These craft range in size from charter boats less than 40 feet in length and a six-man capacity, to a 113-foot super deluxe sportfisher.

The private boat owner's interest in ocean fishing has similarly mushroomed. Of small craft alone, an estimated 68,000 boats less than 16 feet in length made use of coastal waters in 1962, undertaking 780,000 ocean trips and carrying three passengers per trip for approximately 2.3 million activity days.

Private boat participation in the 1970s has increased multifold. In 1975, there were 513,582 registered private boats over 8 feet long in California. While it is impossible to accurately determine how many of those were used for ocean sportfishing, some officials believe as high as 40 percent may be involved and that over one million people fish from those boats in salt water. Another 650,000 fishermen ride Southland partyboats each year.

As interest in ocean fishing and its facilities have both increased, the tools of the trade have improved. Calcutta poles, knuckle-buster reels, linen lines, wire leaders, and large hooks became outmoded as the fish grew wiser under heavier fishing pressure. Gear refinements brought monofilament lines, smaller hooks, reels with complex drag systems, and fiberglass rods manufactured under exacting design standards. Electronic fish finders found their way onto both partyboats and private boats. And a constant stream of lures continues to enter the market, each successive one designed to further capitalize on knowledge being gathered from an ever-expanding science of fishing.

What will Southern California offshore fishing be like a decade from now? The answer depends largely on management of the sport. For one thing, the problem of heavy sportfishing of certain dwindling species will have to be offset by realistic bag limits designed to perpetuate and increase their populations. Our precious anchovy resource—the last remaining significant source of forage fish for most of our offshore game fish that has not yet been overexploited by commercial fishing—will have to be protected from those who use large purse-seine nets and, unfortunately, measure conservation in tonnage dollars earned. And we must all come to realize that although the ocean contains a multitude of renewable resources, these resources do have finite limits, and that as long as we respect the balance of nature and do not overharvest we can enjoy productive recreational ocean fishing for generations to come.

The modern partyboat usually has a large galley with seating for several passengers at a time, roomy bunks, lots of stern fishing space, and the latest in lifesaving and electronic fish-finding equipment. Bait tanks are capable of holding several dozen scoops of live anchovies.

1

Gear That's Fit to Fish With

A chapter on proper tackle logically comes first in a book on fishing because *good* tackle is the foundation upon which all the advanced fishing skills are built. That statement may sound commonplace, even trite, yet at least half of the ocean angling sins I see committed are due primarily to a fisherman's either not understanding what tackle he needs, or else not being willing to invest a few additional dollars in quality gear.

What happens with cheap gear? Rods break at the ferrule or just above the butt section; snap-swivels come part; reel drags freeze up; lines break at the slightest hint of fraying; hooks bend open. In such events, unprintable language is sometimes bellowed by fishermen who rationalize they are merely victims of "bad luck."

A fisherman with a well-built, properly selected rod can whip an albacore or yellowtail in half the time it takes another angler to land the same-size fish on cheap tackle. Quality reels have drag mechanisms that work longer, require less maintenance, and produce smoother pressure on a running fish than do cut-rate reels. First-rate monofilament fishing line is more costly to produce, hence more costly to purchase. But when you consider that the loss of a trophy-size fish through line breakage can be even more costly to you, quality line becomes a bargain.

Ask yourself if you want to become a really good, consistent catcher of fish. In a sense, proficient saltwater fishing is a discipline, and that discipline begins with equipment. Imagine Catfish Hunter buying a $5 baseball glove to snare line drives, or Jack Nicklaus using a beginner's golf club for 30-foot putts, or Billy Sims running through a wave of tacklers while wearing a $10 helmet. The importance of buying the finest gear you can afford—even if it means putting off a purchase until funds are accumulated—just can't be overstressed. Quality tackle produces quality performance. Period.

Conventional Tackle

"Conventional" tackle in saltwater fishing refers to a rod with baitcasting-type guides and a reelseat that accepts the reel on top of the rod butt section, plus a revolving spool reel. In contrast, spinning tackle incorporates a rod with larger-diameter spinning guides and a reelseat that holds the reel *below* the butt section of the rod, plus a stationary spool reel which is designed to let the line coil off the spool during a cast.

Conventional rod and reel outfits have been in use here since the late 1800s, while spinfishing tackle enjoyed its first significant popularity in the United States following World War II.

The advantages of spinning tackle are at least twofold. First, the gear is readily adaptable to beginning fishermen, often allowing at least adequate casts to be made after just a few minutes of instruction. Since the reel bail mechanism and the in-and-out motion of the spool stem combine to automatically guide the line on the reel spool during a retrieve, a fisherman doesn't need an "educated thumb" to lay the line evenly back on the spool. Spinning equipment also allows relatively inexperienced anglers to make casts of decent distances, something that requires some patience and practice (and fighting backlashes) with conventional gear. Second, because of its light tackle design, spinning gear provides grand sport for some of the smaller saltwater species.

One of the inherent disadvantages of spinning gear, however, is that some fishermen find it so attractive that they *never* progress to conventional tackle. Spinning gear, they most probably reason, is so convenient and easy to use that the more demanding skills of conventional rod-and-reeling aren't attempted. Don't fall into this trap. The ultimate rewards of conventional gear are great.

If selecting quality gear is my first saltwater fishing commandment, learning to also use conventional rods and reels is the second. (On the subject of commandments: In this book I am going to relate what I've seen in some 25 years of fishing off Southern California. I intend to present the information in a straightforward manner. That means opinions, and my recommendations.)

I feel that spinning gear provides the utmost fun when fishing for smaller species such as bonito, barracuda, and bass, but that heavier, more rugged types of fishing—from albacore and yellowtail up to marlin and giant tuna—call for conventional outfits. It is possible to catch, say, a 40-pound yellowtail on a light spinning outfit—if the reel holds enough line, if enough pressure can be put on the fish with the light outfit, if the hook doesn't wear a large hole in the fish's mouth before the battle is over, if the lighter line isn't frayed on the bottom of the boat or on another angler's line. And that's too many ifs for me.

In short, conventional outfits generally allow more pressure to be put on a hooked fish; they perform longer under heavy fishing; their reels hold more (and heavier) line; and their reel drag mechanisms are more reliable.

The Conventional Rod

A multitude of choices are available to a fisherman about to purchase a saltwater fishing rod. Just walk into a well-stocked sporting goods store and behold the forest of fish catchers lining the racks. Some rods, I know, are designed to perform admirably and catch fish. Others, I suspect, are designed to catch fishermen.

What to look for in a good rod? There are some universal qualities I consider.

First, you have your choice of a one-piece or two-piece (or more) rod. The advantage of a two-piece rod is obvious; it can be stowed or carried in a smaller space. If space were my only consideration, then, I would have a garageful of two-piece rods.

On the other hand, a one-piece rod means that, on quality rods, the rod blank (the main fiberglass shaft) is one continuous piece of spun fiberglass all the way from the inside of the rod tiptop guide down to the rod butt cap. This translates into *continuous* strength. Many times if a two-piece rod breaks, it snaps at the ferrule, the section that joins the two pieces together. This is because a metal ferrule cannot flex like the rest of the rod, and the ferrule becomes a mini-vise gripping the rod while a fish is bending the shaft. True, advances have been made recently in the form of fiberglass ferrules that do flex with the action of the rod, but my personal selection remains the one-piece model. A one-piece rod of comparable quality will *never* be weaker than a two-piecer, and will often be stronger.

I would especially avoid two-piece boat rods that feature a wooden butt section. Unlike rods with the blank running the entire length of the rod, rods with solid wood butts place an undue stress on the point where the fiberglass rod blank ends at the reelseat. Sometimes when a very large fish is hooked, the rod will break apart at the foregrip or just behind the reelseat. No flex, no give, no fish, no rod remaining. And one partyboat skipper I know has seen so many wooden-butt rods snapped off in trolling rod holders that he has strung a collection of the butts—clothesline fashion —near his wheelhouse on the boat, to serve as a reminder to other fishermen.

Okay, we've got a one-piece rod with a cork or composition type butt section. Now for length. In the past decade, the shift has been away from 9- to 10-foot rods and to 5½- to 7-foot rods. The shorter rods are lighter, handle more easily, are less tiring through a day's fishing, and let you enjoy a better "feel" of the fish you're fighting. The worst tackle purchase I made in my early teens was a rod 12 feet long. It was horrible. It was too long for my 5-foot 8-inch, 150-pound frame to cast comfortably—with any semblance of co-ordination—at that time. On a crowded partyboat I couldn't let enough line hang from the tip to make a graceful cast, because the rod endangered other fishermen standing a dozen feet away. And since the rod was so long, I practically had to stand on the port side of a boat in order to have a fish gaffed on the starboard side.

As a general rule, stick with the shorter rods. You'll be much happier. Even under those occasional circumstances when a longer rod may be required to reach boat-shy fish, I still don't go above an 8-footer these days.

Look for a rod on which a hard finish is applied evenly and adequately covering the rod windings used to hold the guides on the rod. Cheaper rods usually have only a very thin coating of rod varnish or clear resin over the windings; quality rods are subjected to several coats that produce a *smooth*, mirrorlike finish on the winding threads. If you can run your thumbnail over the rod windings and *feel* the individual wraps of the thread, the finish of the rod probably isn't going to stand more than a season of hard fishing.

Other features of a topnotch fishing rod include hard-chromed guides, rod tiptop, and reelseat; a double-ring locking reelseat; comfortably cushioned butt cap, double-wrapped guides and a foregrip section large enough to accept two hands there to lift a large fish.

No single rod, of course, is going to work well under a variety of fishing conditions. Said another way, there is no such thing as an all-purpose fishing rod.

The reasons for this can be seen if rods are compared to golf clubs or baseball gloves. Different clubs are designed to function best at certain distances, or for certain types of shots (chips, putts, and so forth). Likewise, a first baseman's glove is designed differently from a catcher's mitt, because scooping up low throws differs from continually collecting pitches. If you want to improve your saltwater fishing score and you limit yourself to one rod, you are hindering your performance as much as by carrying just a putter or only a driver on a golf course.

How many rod and reel outfits do you need? As a *basic* set, I recommend at least three. You need a light-action live-bait rod to be used with, say 12- and 15-pound test lines; a medium-action designed live-bait rod coupled with 20- or 25-pound line; and a third outfit consisting of a medium-action jig rod (a "jig rod" has a somewhat stiffer tip section and large diameter butt section for use in casting artificial lures) capable of handling 30- to 50-pound test lines.

It is difficult to describe the design differences among light-action, medium-action, heavy-action, jig rod, and so forth, because they involve rod diameters, flexing curves, rod wall thicknesses, and other technical (and boring) specifications. Suffice it to say that any well-stocked sporting goods or tackle store handles all types, and knowledgeable salesmen can show you the difference. Or you can go shopping with a friend who is familiar with the different types. Another way to decide on your choices is to consult a partyboat skipper or crew member.

As for name brands, two of the most notable currently on the market in Southern California include saltwater rods manufactured by the Fenwick Tackle Company (the new Fenwick Pacificstiks, especially) and Sabre rods (check out the Sabre "Stroker" series).

Conventional Reels

My personal choices in conventional ocean fishing reels include those reels made by the Penn Reel Company, Daiwa and Carl Newell (the Newell reels). All of these are quality products offered at reasonable prices and they are backed by good warranties. With minimal maintenance you'll get years of service from the investment made in purchasing these name brands. If you're supplied with a warranty card (as with the Newells), be sure to fill it out and mail it to the manufacturer.

Here's a list of reels I like for different purposes:

Live-bait fishing: Penn 500 SL, Daiwa models 30H and 50H, Newell models 235, 332 and 338.

Jig (lure) fishing: Penn 500 SL, Daiwa models 30H and 50H, Newell 338FJ, Penn 113H converted to narrower width via Newell Yellowtail Special conversion kit, Penn 349H for deep-water yo-yo jigging.

Heavy trolling: Penn 114H, Daiwa 450H and 650H, International 50W.

Bottomfishing (rockfishing): Daiwa 450H and 650H, Penn 114H.

If you'd like more information about these reels, write: Penn Reel Company, 3028 W. Hunting Park Avenue, Philadelphia, PA 19132; Daiwa Corporation, 14011 S. Normandie Avenue, Gardena, CA 90247; Carl Newell Manufacturing, Fishing Tackle Division, 940 Allen Avenue, Glendale, CA 91201. You can also inspect reel catalogs describing various models and their uses at various tackle shops and sporting goods stores throughout Southern California.

Some reels (like the Squidders and Jigmasters) offer a choice of plastic or metal spools when purchased. The plastic spools are lighter in weight but not as strong as metal spools, so are best adaptable to light tackle fishing when longer casts are necessary. Since the metal spool weighs more, it has more inertia to overcome at the beginning of a cast, and more friction to resist during a cast.

On the other hand, when fishing for large fish or when casting heavy jigs, a metal spool's strength makes it superior to a plastic spool. Here's a rule of thumb: Select plastic spools for fishing for bonito, bass, barracuda,

Monofilament lines can produce tremendous constricting pressure on a reel-spool arbor, as evidenced by this reel, which experienced a blownout sideplate when the spool cracked and "popped" or expanded.

small yellowtail, small albacore, and other species of similar size; select a metal spool for heavy line jig fishing, bottomfishing, or fishing for large yellowtail, albacore, tuna, and so forth, when large baits are used.

Note: monofilament line can exert a great constricting pressure on a reel spool arbor (the spool "spindle") when the line stretches under the powerful pull of a heavy fish. Unless some form of backing is used on the reel spool, this pressure can actually crack plastic spools (sometimes called "exploding" or "blowing" the reel spool). When filling a plastic spool with mono, at least 30 yards of backing should first be wound on the spool. The backing may consist of dacron line, old cotton line which is wound on and then taped down (with the mono attached to it as if it were the arbor) or simply building up a thickness of medical adhesive tape to help cushion the spool arbor.

A Glendale, California, manufacturer is now offering several custom-made reel components designed to fit Penn reels. Among the items offered by Carl Newell Manufacturing (6735 San Fernando Road, Glendale, CA 91201) are aluminum spools, reel bars, and reelseats. This system of components is really worth looking into, since it allows you to *increase* the line capacity and (through closer machine tolerances) casting distance of several stock Penn reels, while *decreasing* the weight of the unit. Ask a sporting goods or tackle salesman to show you the "Newellie Spool" and other components and you can judge for yourself.

Spinning Tackle

Since spinfishing is relatively easy to learn, there has been a large boom in spinfishing gear in the past three decades. I feel, however, that its role in offshore ocean fishing is limited primarily to light tackle work with live bait or relatively small lures, and, at that, is best suited to the smaller species of fish.

The same principles of workmanship should be considered in purchasing spinning gear as in purchasing conventional rods and reels. Otherwise, you can buy a rod, reel, line, and a lot of misery and frustration for $25.

Bass, bonito, barracuda, small yellowtail, and other fish lend themselves well to spinning tackle, especially if the fisherman is after the utmost sport from lesser-size fish. Indeed, sometimes the fish can become so spooky and hook-shy that spinfishermen using 10-, 8-, or 6-pound lines and correspondingly small hooks have the advantage. For many types of inshore (surf and bay) fishing, too, spinning tackle performs admirably.

Very light spinning gear used aboard a private boat, where the fishing group is small and friendly, can really be fun. It takes a certain amount of skill and expertise to land, say, a 10-pound bonito on only 4-pound test line and, when fishing from a private boat, the boat can be used to follow

Spinning tackle is best suited for smaller species. This 8-pound bonito proved to be a sporty adversary on medium-class spinning gear.

the fish if necessary, so that the fisherman doesn't run out of line. On the other hand, very light spin tackle often *does not* belong on a crowded partyboat, because it usually takes much longer to land a fish. Consider what happens if a light tackle artist hooks up just a few minutes before the partyboat skipper was going to move the craft and its 49 other passengers to a different fishing spot. Everyone else must wait for some time while one man fights a fish.

Spinning Rods

About spinning rods there is little to say that has not already been said about conventional rods. Again, a one-piece rod is recommended and, for spinning, one that is from 5½ to 6½ feet in length. If I had to choose one spinning outfit that would be most versatile (assuming the fisherman also has some conventional outfits) I would advise a 5½-foot, fast taper, medium-light action rod capable of handling a range of 6- to 12-pound test lines. Even with such a light rod I would still select a model that has room for both hands on its foregrip, a definite asset in applying pressure when lifting on a large fish—which will sometimes be hooked on spinfishing gear when you least expect it.

Spinning rods with flex-type guides are also advised. The "feet" of the rod guides are made of spring metal so that they bend with the arc of the rod, in contrast to the braced guides, which do not give with the rod. The flexing allows the rod to produce a more even pressure as it bends, lessening the chance of breakage.

Spinning Reels

A good saltwater spinning reel *must* have a strong, smooth-functioning reel drag, since such light lines are used (usually no more than 20-pound test, and usually under 15-pound test). For general light-tackle fishing, the reel should hold at least 200 yards of 10-pound test; for medium-class spinfishing, at least 200 yards of 20-pound test.

It should be noted that one of the frequent errors made by beginning fishermen using spin equipment is turning the reel handle while the fish is running or stationary. Because of the method of retrieving the line with the bail mechanism on a spin reel, this only results in badly twisting the line. *Never* try to reel in a fish when it is running or sulking in one spot. Retrieve line (using the pumping method, which we'll talk about later) only when you feel that the fish is sufficiently tired out to be moved toward you and you can *gain* line.

A big advantage in a saltwater spinning reel is a quick-change spool system. Some reels feature pushbutton spools that allow you to pop off one

Even ultralight spinning tackle has a place in ocean fishing—when used on private boats where lots of time can be taken, if necessary, to land a fish without bothering other fishermen. This large sand bass fell victim to a feather and only 4-pound test line.

spool and snap on another in a matter of seconds. Thus, with three different spools of 6-, 8-, and 12-pound test line—or 8-, 10-, and 12-pound line if you want to narrow the range—you have in essence three different fishing outfits which can be quickly converted.

Among the better choices in ocean spin reels are those manufactured by Garcia (their old standby the Mitchell with fast retrieve ratio is one of the fishermen's favorites), plus the Quick Corporation and the Penn Reel Company.

By the way, the International Spin Fishing Association was for years based in Southern California and kept world-record catches for spinfishing (up to 12-pound test line). This function has recently been transferred to the International Game Fish Association (IGFA), which also maintains world records for freshwater and saltwater fish taken on conventional, revolving-spool tackle. Information about IGFA records and memberships may be obtained by writing: IGFA, 3000 East Las Olas Boulevard, Fort Lauderdale, FL 33316.

Fishing Line

Except for some instances of trolling for marlin or deep-water bottom-fishing for rockfish, line for offshore use in the Southland region means monofilament line.

Actually, the fisherman has only two things to consider when buying monofilament line: (1) purchasing the strength (pound test) of line he desires, which is easy since all lines are labelled; and (2) buying a high-quality line, sometimes not so easy if you're not willing to pay the price.

Buying line is, however, like purchasing almost anything else: You get what you pay for. And for cheap line you'll pay dearly in lost fish. Indeed, your fishing line is virtually the only thing separating you from your fish; it is the vital link connecting hook or lure to rod and reel. A poorly manufactured line will have too little or too much stretch; will not have good chafe resistance; will not lay smoothly on the reel; will not be supple enough for easy casting; will have inferior visibility qualities; and will break under less strain than a quality line of the same stated pound test strength.

What are some good brands of lines? My favorite is Maxima, a German-made line imported and distributed locally throughout Southern California at sporting goods outlets. I've also had very good results with Meslon and Ande lines, a couple of other imports, but "Max," as the veterans call it, remains my first choice.

Most lines are offered in bulk spools of many hundreds of yards, and you should consider buying it in these larger quantities. Bulk line is usually cheaper per hundred yards than single or connected 100-yard spools. If you buy bulk line you can fill your reels exactly to the full mark with no waste, which cannot be done with the connected 100-yard spools. Say, for example, that your reel holds 270 yards of 25-pound test and you purchase three connected 100-yard spools. You have 30 yards of waste, unless you like to restring tennis rackets.

Heat is one of the worst enemies of monofilament line, so never store your line in a hot place. If you leave bulk spools of line in the garage, insulate them by wrapping a piece of tinfoil around the spools. You'll be surprised how much longer your mono stays fresh.

When filling a reel spool, always apply a slight tension to the line so that it packs properly on the spool and won't tend to backlash on the first cast. By the way, a dry line is always more susceptible to backlash than a wet one; so when you begin fishing don't try to achieve your ultimate distance on the first few casts. Instead, make the first few casts of moderate distance until the line becomes wet and therefore packs together better on the spool. When using a conventional reel, it's necessary to guide the line back and forth evenly on the spool, using your left thumb. An unevenly laid line invites burned thumbs (on the cast), backlashes, and line piled so high in one spot that it may rub on the inside of the reel and keep the spool from turning.

Line ages, and the speed of its aging depends partly on how often you fish. Worn-out line can become brittle, develop a coil-set, oxidize, and break under little pressure. There are no exacting rules for when to change line, but as a guideline:

If you fish occasionally, say three or four times a season, change *at least once* a season;

If you fish frequently, about every other weekend, change *at least twice* a season;

If you fish several times a month, virtually every chance you get, you may have to change your line *monthly or even more frequently*.

The early albacore season is notorious for revealing who is fishing with good line and who is trying to get by without changing his line. The first action of the season is usually signaled by a chorus of cracks like rifle shots, as old lines snap here and there, leaving their victims wishing they had invested a few dollars on fresh mono before the trip.

Monofilament lines can become quickly frayed when rubbed against the hull of a boat or when tangled with other lines, so it's important to frequently check the condition of your line when fishing. If there is any questionable portion, cut back the line to what you know to be good line. The greatest wear occurs in the last three to five feet of line when casting with heavy jigs or fighting large fish, since this section continually passes back and forth through the rod tip. After landing several good-size fish, it's a good idea to cut off this section and start again with fresh line.

Knots can also weaken after several fish have been boated, so make it a practice to cut back a few inches of the line and retie the hook occasionally. Even though the line may not look frayed, it can be weak.

Dacron line has a limited use, but is a good choice when trolling for marlin, sailfish, and other big game varieties, or when deep-water rockfishing at depths of over 200 feet (and down as far as 800 feet at times). Here it is vital that stretch is minimal; you want to drive the hook sharply and immediately into a tough-mouthed marlin, and, at trolling distance, there can be too much stretch in monofilament to properly set the hook. Likewise, if you lift the rod tip three feet to set the hook into a deep water rockfish, by the time that force is carried through the inherent stretch of 500 feet of monofilament line you may be lucky to move the hook an inch. Remember, when you don't want stretch, use dacron.

Terminal Tackle

Broadly defined, terminal tackle is anything that is tied on the end of the line, including snap swivels, wire leaders, snaps, jigs (lures) and sinkers. For the vast majority of Southern California offshore fishing, the only terminal gear required is hooks, sinkers, and jigs.

The most popular and generally effective type of sinker in this area is the rubbercore sinker. This consists of a lead torpedo-shaped sinker with a slot running down the length of its middle and two rubber tabs protruding from each end. Easy to put on and remove, the rubbercore sinker is attached simply by slipping the line into the sinker slot and then twisting each end tab a few turns around the line. A rubbercore can be attached or unfastened on monofilament line in about five seconds. Its obvious advantage is that different weights can be changed so quickly to suit fishing conditions. A less obvious, yet important advantage is that no knot is required to attach the sinker, hence there is no loss of line strength. (A knot, no matter how tied, is always weaker than the unknotted portion of the line.)

Rubbercore sinkers come in a variety of sizes from about 1/16-ounce to 2 ounces. Weights from ½- to 1½-ounces are, however, the most commonly used. Be sure you have a good supply of rubbercores in your tackle box.

A larger sinker should be used when fishing deep with large baits such as mackerel or squid. Under these circumstances, the best type is a torpedo-shaped sinker with a ring eye at each end, to which the line is tied. Because of its streamlined shape this sinker is less likely to hang up in rocks, and because of the ring eyes at each end it gives a direct line pull on a hooked fish.

By far the most frequently used type of hook for offshore fishing is a short-shank, single-point O'Shaughnessy-type hook often referred to locally as a "live-bait" or "tuna" hook. Both Eagle Claw and Mustad make quality hooks of this type. They are available in either a nickel or bronze finish, but I feel I've had significantly better results using the nickel finish, since it seems to be less visible in clear water.

The accompanying chart shows the actual sizes of the most frequently used live bait hooks.

Hook-size Chart

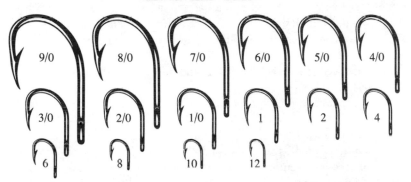

Sizes of live-bait style O'Shaughnessy-type hooks most commonly used off Southern California.

There are actually three considerations in selecting a given size hook—
the size of the fish sought, the size of the bait being used, and the feeding
mood of the fish. Generally, the larger the fish and the larger the bait, the
larger the hook selected, but, if the fish are not hitting aggressively, you
may have to drop to a smaller (less visible) hook to get a strike.

As a rule, medium-size live anchovies are pinned on size 2 or 4 hooks.
Anchovies less than four inches long, however, may require the use of a
size 6 hook. Extremely large anchovies may allow the use of a size 1.

When live squid or mackerel are used for bait, hooks ranging from size
1/0 to 4/0 can be used, even up to a size 6/0 in a wild, hot feeding spree.
Keep in mind, though, if you're fishing for yellowtail or other fish and are
using live squid for bait, and the fish seem finicky, dropping down to a
smaller size 1 or 2 hook may interest the fish enough for them to strike.

Bluefin tuna are perhaps the most keen-eyed and cautious fish of all in
our waters, so very small hooks are usually necessary. Even with a good-
size anchovy for bait, a size 6 or 8 hook is most appropriate. Hooks of this
size have less holding power than larger hooks, for sure, but it's better to
get hooked up and play your fish gingerly, risking a bent-open or pulled
out hook, than never to draw a strike at all.

A general guide to remember is that smaller hooks usually produce
more strikes and allow the bait to swim in a more natural, unhindered
manner. But using small hooks means you suffer a loss in holding power
and tensile strength. The suggestions I've given above represent a happy
compromise.

As for snap-swivels, wire leaders, and other paraphernalia on the line
—forget them. In the days of Zane Grey our local sport fish would accept
such hardware, but no more. Game fish populations have responded to
ever-increasing angling pressure by becoming more "educated"; they shun
anything too unnatural on the line. There are still some who believe, for
instance, that wire leaders should be used in barracuda fishing, since the
fish have sharp teeth. That's fine if you *hook* a barracuda, but I would
rather that two out of three hooked barracuda cut the line than to fish all
day with an unmolested bait. Straight monofilament line draws more
strikes—so many more that you'll end up hooking and landing more fish
without wire leaders.

Jigs are used effectively, however, and they will be discussed in subse-
quent chapters.

Accessory Equipment

In addition to rods, reels, lines, hooks, sinkers, and jigs, several other
pieces of accessory equipment can make you a better, or at least more comfortable, fisherman.

For years, the most popular and practical tackle boxes for ocean fishing were those big, rectangular shaped wooden boxes made of marine plywood. They are still my favorites simply because I like the looks of natural wood, but during the past half-dozen years several ABS plastic tackle boxes have been introduced that are more than adequate for the deep sea fisherman.

Size is important in a tackle box. It is far better to buy a box that is *too large* for your current needs, so that as you add tackle you can grow into your box. If you buy a box only large enough to hold your present gear, you may end up with an undersize and unusable tackle toter in the near future.

A good tackle box should be roomy enough to accommodate at least three dozen jigs, several boxes of hooks, an assortment of rubbercore sinkers, diagonal cutters, fish towels, extra reel spools, trolling feathers, bait knife, whet stone, pliers, screwdriver, small can of aerosol lubricant, a spare reel or two, and bulk spools of line, to name just some of the items. The box should contain enough individual compartments so that this gear can be logically separated and found in a hurry. If you have to hunt through a mess in your box while everyone else is getting hooked up, your tackle box is actually losing you fish. And believe me, it does happen.

If you are considering undertaking one of those multiday, long-range sportfishing trips that depart from San Diego and fish off Baja California, you may want to consider owning a smaller "local" tackle box and a larger "long-range" box. When you're on a long-range trip it's a long walk to the tackle store (about 1000 miles from the tip of Baja).

To economize a little on space, it's a good idea to purchase a small, compartmented, clear plastic box to hold all your hooks. These boxes measure about 3½ inches wide and 8 inches long and have about eight individual compartments. Thus you can keep eight different sizes of hooks in a single container; you won't have to search out eight different tiny boxes just to get at a hook.

And to save unnecessary trips to the tackle box, which can cost you valuable fishing time, slip a few hooks of the size you'll most probably be using, along with a few rubbercore sinkers, into your shirt or jacket pocket when you get aboard the boat. If you need to change, you can do it without leaving your fishing spot.

Another necessary piece of gear is a good pair of longnose pliers, to extract hooks from landed fish. Stanley Tools makes a heavy-duty set that will last for years. You should also have a leather belt holster to carry the pliers with you when fishing. Don't, however, spend needless time trying to pry out a hook if it is deep in a fish. In the process, you'll probably damage the hook and, besides, hooks are cheap (one of the few quality items in fishing gear that are cheap), so don't waste the time.

Always remember to remove your pliers when you sit in an upholstered booth or lie in your bunk on a boat. Those handles have a way of wiggling around and playing havoc with upholstery.

Also recommended is a set of diagonal cutters for cutting monofilament line. Some fishermen like to simply use fingernail clippers, but I've found these dull sooner, or come apart, or get very rusty. They are also difficult to grasp when your hands are wet or when the weather is cold. Two-handled diagonals are much easier to grip, they last longer and work much better on heavy line, since great leverage can be applied with them.

Besides their use in tying or retying hooks and sinkers, diagonal cutters will get you out of a bad line tangle in a hurry. It's much better to excuse yourself and cut yourself out of a bad tangle than to wait around for someone to undo the mess. Why wait, when all you're going to lose is a few feet of line? (You can usually reclaim the hook and sinker or jig from the tangle.) Yet I've seen fishermen stand around doggedly and wait to be worked out of a veritable spider web, when those fishing are hooking a fish with every cast. Then, by the time the tangle is undone, the fish may have left.

Fishing boats can be wet places, and nothing makes you (or me, anyway) quite as miserable as fishing with wet feet. To prevent this, a lot of veteran ocean fishermen, especially those aboard partyboats, wear shorty-type rubber boots. The shorties can be purchased at many sporting goods stores, commercial fishing supply houses, and most partyboat landings. If you don't wear shorties, the ways to get wet feet are numerous: from deckhands hosing down the deck between fishing stops; from water washing on the deck during rough weather; from live-bait tanks plugging up and overflowing on the deck.

A disadvantage of shorty boots is that they get warm in warm weather, but an occasional outside wetting usually eliminates the problem.

Next to shorty boots, tennis shoes are probably the best choice. They do get wet, but at least they have beefy tread designs (like shorties) to help prevent you from falling on a slippery deck. Once wet, tennis shoes take a long time to dry, so on an extended trip I'd consider taking two pairs.

Fish towels are often overlooked, but are certainly handy to take along. All species of saltwater fish possess a degree of slime which serves as a protective outer coating, and handling fish is bound to leave you with "fishy" hands. Barracuda, halibut, and wahoo are among the slimiest. Tear some strips of terrycloth about a foot wide and three feet long and tuck them away in your tackle box and you'll be prepared to keep your hands clean. You'll also find you're the most popular guy on the boat, because no one else thought to bring any towels.

Another good piece of accessory equipment, which is really a necessary piece of equipment when fighting large fish, is the leather rod-butt belt.

A fisherman uses a cross-strap type of reel harness to aid him in fighting a large fish. The full-shoulder harness is preferred, however, since it tends to distribute the strain more broadly over the fisherman's back and shoulders.

Rod butt belts feature a large, semitriangular piece of heavy leather and a butt "cup" that is held in front of your abdominal area by a waist belt. The unit provides comfort and protection to your abdomen while giving you a place to rest the rod butt while fighting a fish. It isn't necessary to use a rod-butt belt when fishing for smaller fish or, in some cases, even when fishing for a *few* large fish, but if you expect to catch many large fish I'd advise using this device.

A good rod-butt belt will last for years, providing you occasionally go over it with saddle soap to clean and preserve the leather. Look for a model that has a relatively thick belt section that will not wear out prematurely. When you wear your rod-butt belt, you can attach your diagonal pliers holster, longnose pliers holster, and fish towels to it.

Fighting very large fish such as black sea bass, marlin, yellowfin tuna, and broadbill swordfish can call for the use of a vest harness, unless you have the luxury of a fighting chair. Unless you specialize in fishing for these species, however, chances are your harness won't see much use. On the other hand, if you undertake a long-range Baja trip, the harness becomes a necessity, since large, hard-fighting species are common.

The vest harness is worn, as its name implies, like a vest. It has straps running horizontally around the angler's shoulders and lower back and attaching in front to the fishing reel, allowing the fisherman to use his back muscles and to at least partially rest his arms and wrists during an extended battle. When the rod butt is positioned in the cup of a rod-butt belt and the straps of the vest harness are snapped onto the reel lugs, it's possible for the fisherman to hold up his fishing outfit without even using his hands. When fighting a big fish, the fisherman wearing a harness vest need exert his arms only when lifting or pumping a fish; when the rod remains steady while the fish is running or sulking, the harness takes a good share of the work.

Clothing may seem relatively insignificant as accessory equipment, but it should not be overlooked. First, wear clothes that are expendable, since fishing can get messy. Second, it is better to overdress in chilly weather and peel off clothes to suit the temperature, than to dress too lightly and suffer. A hat with some sort of brim will help decrease eye fatigue caused by a bright sun (or even a bright overcast day); sunglasses aid the same purpose. They also add a degree of protection, for more than one stray hook has luckily whisked off a hat or a pair of glasses instead of finding flesh.

I like to carry with me as much tackle as is practical when I'm fishing, so I select old shirts and jackets that have roomy pockets.

Finally, if you expect rainy weather, don't forget to bring along a rain slicker or parka. Wet is not beautiful.

2

The Basics: Proper Techniques

A fisherman can be beautifully outfitted with the finest equipment, but if he doesn't know how to properly *use* his gear, he's going to have a lot of disappointing days offshore.

I once saw a guy using a $70 rod (and 70 bucks was a lot of money then, about 20 years ago), trying to fight a 50-pound yellowtail. He made the mistake of resting the rod on the handrail of the boat, immediately creating a fulcrum or area of strain on the rod, against which the fish could pull. The rod snapped like a broom handle and it was only sheer luck that the yellow had been tired enough that it could be handlined in to the boat. Similarly, I've witnessed inept anglers make a shambles out of $300 fishing reels and not catch a fish on some of the most expensive lures made, because they didn't know what to do once they *hooked* a fish.

Learning the basics of saltwater fishing is as fundamental—and necessary—as learning to crawl before you walk.

Casting

He who casts well is well on his way to becoming a good fisherman. On the other hand, if you can only cast 30 feet, your fishing activity is *limited* to fishing no more than 360 inches away from your rod tip, a situation that does not promise immense satisfaction when the fish lie 100 feet from the boat. The poor caster is also going to spend a lot of time picking out backlashes in his reel when others are fishing; he is going to miss his target by several yards when an accurate cast may be necessary to reach fish boiling on the surface; he is bound to do relatively poorly in using artificial lures, unless the fish are in a mood to bite a jig dropped straight down over the side.

Casting, then, is extremely important. But before we discuss three different types of casts, let's take a look at a critical note of safety.

I'm not trying to be gruesome, but I am going to be factual. In some 20 years of ocean fishing I've seen hooks deeply imbedded in buttocks, arms, wrists, legs, cheeks (that was a nasty one), backs, eyes (a terrible tragedy) and a score of fingers. Shamefully, virtually all of these mishaps could have been prevented if some fishermen had exercised more caution and common sense when casting.

Always check behind you to see that no one is standing where they could possibly be stuck by your hook(s) when you make a cast.

You should *never* take your eyes off your bait or lure until it hits the water. The proper and safe way to cast is to watch your hook(s) behind you, then turn your head *after* you start coming forward with the cast. If you don't watch your hook(s) behind you, a person could suddenly step near your rod tip and get hooked. Fishing is an exciting sport and the "other guy" isn't always alert to what you are doing, so take special care not to needlessly injure anyone.

Conventional Casting

With conventional fishing gear the principal cast to be mastered is the overhand cast, which is used more than 90 percent of the time when surface fishing. Here's how it's accomplished:

To begin, hold the butt section of the rod, under the reel, with the right hand. Using your right thumb, hold the reel spool stationary, while you use your left hand to flip the freespool lever into the freespool position on the reel. Now move your left hand near the end of the rod butt. Your body weight should be shifted to the right foot, which is about 18 inches behind your left foot and pointing away from your body at about a 45-degree angle. Your left foot faces forward toward the target and your body should be at about a right angle to the target.

To start the cast from this stance, extend the rod back and away from your body, but in line with your target. Swing the rod tip up and forward, increasing the force applied to the cast as the tip comes forward and pivoting your shoulders and hips toward the target. It may sound a bit complicated, but it isn't; watch a good caster and you'll see how gracefully and effortlessly a proper cast is achieved.

When the rod is vertical, or nearly so, allow the bait or jig to pull line from the reelspool by releasing your thumb pressure on the turning spool so you'll avoid a backlash. Similarly, stop the reel spool from turning the instant your bait or lure hits the water.

As the rod moves through its arc during the cast, remember to shift your body weight from your rear foot to your forward foot. Otherwise, you'll be casting from an uncomfortable and inefficient flat-footed stance.

A person who fishes infrequently may require a substantial amount of time to master the overhand cast, unless he practices away from the water, too. As a kid, I spent a lot of afternoons at a large city park, chucking a 2-ounce jig from my rod tip. In a short time, proper casting became second nature. Always begin with *short* casts when learning, don't try to set a record, unless you're pushing for the world's most bizarre backlash. Concentrate on smoothness and form; distance must wait. When casting on dry land, it's best to keep your line wet, too (pour some water over the line occasionally). Dry line has a great tendency to backlash, while wet line packs better and holds together more on the spool.

Casting with Spin Rods

The casting stance and the cast itself are somewhat different for spinning tackle.

To start the overhand spinning cast, begin by facing the target, with the left foot slightly forward of the right. Release the line from the reel by opening the bail mechanism and holding the line with the forefinger of your right hand. The right hand holds the rod just above the reel and the left hand is positioned near the butt of the rod. Swing the rod back in a straight line with the target, increasing the force as the rod nears a vertical position by pulling the rod butt upward with the right hand, and at the same time pushing the butt end downward with the left. This creates a sort of fast, chopping sweep of the rod. As the rod nears a 1 o'clock position the motion is halted abruptly, then reversed so that the right hand snaps the rod back out in front while the left hand sharply pulls the butt end back toward you.

Although the shoulders supply most of the muscle for this snap-type cast, both your knees and hips should pivot slightly back and forward during the procedure. As the rod coming forward nears the vertical position, release the line from your finger.

Note: To properly perform both types of overhand cast, it is necessary to "follow through" with your rod motion as the bait or jig is sailing through the air, much the same as a golfer or tennis player follows through with his swing. Following through will produce the maximum distances and insure that the bait or lure travels on a smooth arc through the air.

Also, the two casting procedures just outlined apply to right-handed casters. If you're left-handed, simply reverse all references to left and right foot, left and right hand, and so forth.

The Underhand Lob

The underhand lob is a simple yet handy cast to know. It is a good choice when fishing in areas where an overhand cast is not possible—for instance, when you have to fish with the superstructure of the boat directly behind you. The underhand lob is also appropriate when the fish are very close to the boat, say, 20 to 40 feet away, when you could actually overshoot the fish with an overhand cast.

Basically the same for either conventional or spinning gear, the underhand cast begins with three or four feet of line hanging down from the rod tip. Then, by lifting and lowering the rod tip, you can swing the bait or jig back and forth pendulum-fashion, gaining momentum with each successive swing. When sufficient speed has been achieved, swing the lure or bait out underhand, releasing the line as the rod nears a horizontal position.

Simple as the underhand cast may be, it requires some practice. The first few attempts are likely to see the line released prematurely, leaving the bait or jig near your feet; or released too late, sending the offering almost straight up in the air. To begin, strive for a smooth swing and for control, allowing distance to develop with practice.

Knowing about Knots

There are two kinds of saltwater fishing knots: good ones, and those that lose you fish. An improperly tied knot *cuts into* the line, thereby defeating its purpose. There are vast multitudes of knots, indeed; one book in my fishing reference library lists some 45 different choices. For most Southern California ocean fishing, however, three knots are most widely used.

Carefully study the accompanying diagrams and learn to quickly and correctly tie these three types of knots. Practice tying them at home, to build up your speed. Sometimes being able to quickly retie a hook during a fast feeding spree can earn you an extra fish.

Never, never use a questionable knot. Cut and retie any knots that you feel may have gathered and formed incorrectly. It only takes a few seconds to tie another knot, but you may not forget for a lifetime a big fish that your knot aided in getting away.

To form an end loop in your fishing line, use the *Perfection Loop*:

1. Take one turn around the monofilament, and hold the crossing between thumb and forefinger.

1.

2. Take a second turn around the crossing, and bring the end around again
   between the turns.

3. Pass Loop B through Loop A.

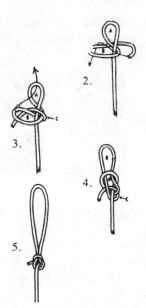

4. Pull this loop up tight until jammed.

5. The finished knot

To join together two pieces of monofilament of approximately the same
diameter, use the *Blood Knot*:

1. Lap the ends of the strands to be
   joined and twist one around the
   other, making at least five turns.
   Count the turns made. Place the
   end between the strands, following
   the arrow.

2. Hold the end against the turns already made, between the thumb and
   forefinger at point marked "X," to
   keep from unwinding. Now wind
   the other short end around the other
   strand for the same number of
   turns, but in the opposite direction.

3. This shows how the knot would
   look if held firmly in place. Actually, as soon as released, the turns
   equalize.

4. And the turns look like this. Now pull on both ends of the monofilaments.

5. As pulling on the ends is continued, the turns gather as above and draw closer together (at this point the short ends may be worked backward, if desired, to avoid cutting off too much of the material).

6. Appearance of the finished knot. All that remains to be done is to cut off the short ends close to the knot.

To tie line to a jig, hook, snap, snap swivel, sinker, or other ring-eyed terminal gear, use the *Improved Clinch Knot*. Properly tied, the improved clinch knot (by far the most commonly used) allows about 95 percent retention of the original, unknotted line strength.

The knot is tied in the following steps:

1. Pass the end of the line through the hook eye, double back and make five or more wraps of the free end of the line around the standing line.
2. Holding the coils, bring the end back through the first loop formed between the coils and the hook eye and then back through the big loop created in the process.
3. Pull slightly on the free end of the line while drawing up the standing end to form the knot.
    (See the two-step drawing below.)

Setting the Reel Drag

One of the chief villains of hooked and liberated fish is the too-tight reel drag. If the drag is set tighter than the line has the strength to withstand, the line will surely break as the fish is running. Conversely, if the reel drag is set too loose, too much needless time will be spent in fighting a fish, and extending the contest just gives the fish more opportunity to escape.

The drag should be set so that maximum pressure can be applied with the rod, yet still just under the breaking point of the line being used. For veteran fishermen, this is largely a matter of "feel," but how can less knowledgeable anglers properly set their drag? One good method is offered here.

Begin by tying the end of your line to a tree, post, car bumper, or other immovable object. Then slowly tighten down on the drag until the maximum amount of pressure can be applied with the arching rod, yet still allowing the line to slip off the reel. Now back off (decrease) the drag slightly from that point, to allow for the inherent increase in drag when your line is pulled through the water.

Until you have learned the "feel" for setting drags (unless you have a scale to set your drag by), it's far better to begin fishing with a drag a little too loose than one a little too tight. The former allows you a margin of adjustment when you hook a fish; the latter may not.

Even though a drag is properly set when a fish is first hooked, it may have to be readjusted during the battle. For example, if the fish pulls several hundred yards of line off the reel, the drag should be decreased or it may break, since a long line moving through the water has an inherent, added drag of its own. You may, for instance, be fishing with a 15-pound drag, but by the time your quarry is pulling 250 yards of line through the water, the pressure on the line is increased several pounds above that mark. Remember, if a fish runs out a long distance from the boat, loosen your drag accordingly. Retighten to the original drag when the fish is brought back closer to the boat.

If too-tight drags bust off a lot of fish, thumbs don't do a bad job, either. A few overly eager fishermen get excited when their fresh-hooked fish is streaking off and, as a result, a thumb or two is clamped down on the reel spool to stop the fish. The result is predictable: a lost fish and nothing to soothe a burned thumb.

Feeling a hook impaled in its mouth and dragging a bunch of monofilament through the water, a hooked fish does not particularly like to be bossed around by a fiberglass rod, so it is going to take defensive action and try to run. In the case of large yellowtail, white sea bass, albacore, and similar species, that run may be several hundred yards, so don't panic. If you're fishing with properly matched equipment and a full spool of line, chances are remote that a fish will take all of the line. Let the rod and reel drag do the work while you enjoy the action.

A few tips on reel maintenance: (1) always rinse off your reels with a freshwater hose after use in saltwater; (2) always back off the drag mechanism when the reels aren't in use; (3) have your reel drag washers replaced at least once a year, sooner if the drag seems to act "jerky"; (4) store your reels in a cloth bag or other covering to keep dust and grit from entering (an old sock is good) and (5) oil your reels periodically, to ensure long life (consult your manual).

Follow Your Hookup

So now you know how to cast and how to set your drag, and you hook a fish and it streaks off. Chances are the fish won't run straight out away from you. More likely it will take off at an angle toward the bow or stern of the boat, and the worst possible thing that can be done at this time is to stand in one place. You have to follow your fish.

Most line tangles occur when a fisherman doesn't keep his hooked fish out in front of him at all times. Trying to handle a hookup from the stern while your fish is thrashing the water off the bow is only inviting a tangled mess involving all of the other fishermen between you and your fish.

The trick to keeping out of line tangles as you follow your fish is to note the position of your line in relation to the other fishermens' lines you must pass. If your line is running out above the fisherman's next to you, simply hold your rod tip high above his rod as you pass behind him, so that the lines won't tangle. On the other hand, if your line is running *below* his line, you must have him step back so that you can pass in front of him. The procedure sounds simple enough, but some beginning fishermen regard another fisherman as an impossible obstacle, or else they feel they'll be inconsiderate if they have to pass behind or under another angler. Actually, they're more inconsiderate if they don't follow their fish.

It's a good idea to alert others that you are moving their way with a hookup, too. Usually, just shouting something like, "Fish on, coming down!" is sufficient. You can't expect a person to stay out of your way if he has his back turned and doesn't even know you exist.

At best, even veteran fishermen find themselves in some tangles. If the tangle is a simple matter of one line wrapping around another, the best thing to do is to *immediately* begin passing your rod around the other person's rod, while his rod remains stationary, even if you can't tell which direction the wraps are occurring. By sheer luck, you'll be right 50 percent of the time. If, after a few passes of rod tip, you find the wrap is getting worse, reverse your direction and in about five or six revolutions you'll find you've unwrapped the tangle.

If there are eight or 10 or more wraps around the lines, the best procedure is to immediately put the rod tips together, step back so that you can get at the lines, and then check to see which direction one rod must be rotated around the other, stationary rod to clear the wraps. Then do it quickly.

Time is of the essence when hooked fish are involved in a tangle, since tangles can cut or burn their way through monofilament lines in scant seconds, especially if the fish is freshly hooked and "hot." Action must be taken to correct a tangle immediately.

Fighting a Fish

A large fish isn't going to be muscled directly in to the boat—it is going to run, to turn, to dash off again, to sulk, sound, and fight you every kick of its tail back to the boat. To tire the fish, the rod must be held high as the fish is running or sulking, then used in a pumping motion to lift the fish toward you as it becomes more fatigued.

When a sizable fish is first hooked, it will not be possible to turn it and retrieve line. The rod tip must be held high, with the *butt section* of the rod at about a 90-degree angle to the line. If, for instance, the fish is fighting straight down, the butt section of the rod should be held on about a horizontal plane, whereas if the fish is far out on the surface, the butt section should be almost vertical. Keeping the rod tip high allows the rod to place maximum pressure on the fish, lets you minimize your work, and allows the rod tip to absorb any sharp strains on the line which would otherwise part the monofilament.

When a rod tip is held low, or a rod is pointed down the line at the fish, there is little or no rod pull against the fish and the pressure on the line is increased. Without the shock absorption of the tip section, the hook can be ripped out of the fish's mouth or the line can break.

The pumping method begins when the fish begins to tire and the angler feels it can be moved by raising the rod tip. By a slow, smooth lift of the rod to a point between 11 o'clock and 12 o'clock, the fish is brought in a few feet toward the fisherman. Then, by a drop of the rod tip just slow enough not to allow any slack in the line and at the same time to allow retrieving, one "pump" of line is gained. The end of the drop should be somewhere between 9 o'clock and 10 o'clock (actually, the bent tip of the rod will be farther down than this).

If you drop the rod tip faster than you can retrieve line, slack will occur and this can allow the hook to slip out of the hole worn in the fish's mouth.

Of course, there's one other small chore when using conventional reels and pumping a fish. The left thumb must be positioned over the front top of the reel so it can guide the line back and forth evenly on the reel spool. There are a few level-wind type reels on the market that will accomplish this, but I wouldn't recommend them; they tend to break down and they also decrease casting distance. In lieu of a level-winder, developing an "educated thumb" takes practice, but if the line is not laid back evenly on the spool it can bunch up so much in one area that the line will rub on the reel bars or reel foot and the spool will no longer revolve. This happens mostly to fishermen who get so excited during a hookup that they forget about guiding the line back on the spool.

(Above) After two trips around the boat, and passing successfully by a lot of other anglers' lines, this yellowtail proves a worthwhile prize for the veteran angler who caught it.

(Left top) This battle ends successfully for the fisherman who used proven saltwater techniques. The fish is a bluefin tuna, taken aboard a small boat during a late-summer run off Redondo Beach.

(Left bottom) A yellowtail comes to gaff at Catalina Island. Care should be taken to let fish lie flat during gaffing; never pull a fish's head out of water when it is going to be gaffed.

It takes some experience to learn the right fishing techniques, but once mastered, the results are shown by this fisherman's beaming smile. The catch is a 30-pound white sea bass.

The Gaffing Stage

Unless a fish is a small one, it will probably have to be gaffed to be brought aboard the boat. The gaffing stage of the fight is one of the most critical; a fish often makes a final burst or two when very close to the surface and a second of panic by the fisherman can result in a break off.

For the most effective gaffing, the fish should be pumped up to a point from a foot to only inches *below* the surface of the water. A fish may *look* close when it's only five or six feet from the surface, but that's still too far below to be gaffed. To make the gaffer's job least difficult, bring the fish up so that its head is just barely under water, let the fish lay flat and sideways and hold it in that position until it is impaled on the gaff hook.

Never lift a fish's head out of water. This takes the fish out of its environment and its reaction is a lot of flopping, thrashing, twisting, and general misbehaving so that the chances are increased you'll lose it right at the boat.

The reel should be immediately placed into freespool once your fish is gaffed and you should hold your thumb lightly on the reel spool. Following this procedure, you won't be faced with a broken line if the fish accidentally falls off the gaff and falls several feet back into the water.

3

Using a Bait that Wiggles

Southern California offshore fishing is principally a *live* bait fishery, hence the chapter title. Contrast this to saltwater fishing in the gulf and Eastern seaboard states, where much dead or cut bait is used. To maintain a Southland live-bait fishery, however, a fleet of live-bait boats must catch bait (most commonly anchovies) year-round to supply the area's party-boats, charter boats, and private boats all along the coast. The partyboats

Using live bait most effectively involves knowing how to select it, handle it, hook it, and fish with it. This bait tank is a small "diaper (canvas) bag" style, commonly seen hanging over the stern of private boats.

are equipped with large live-bait tanks that can hold from a dozen to a couple of hundred scoops of live bait, depending on the size of the craft. In addition, most private boat owners who are serious about ocean fishing also have some capability of holding live bait aboard their vessels.

The Family of Baits

Eight different types of live baits are most commonly used off the Southland coast. By far the most used is the anchovy, followed by squid, mackerel, herring, tomcod, sardines, perch, and pompano.

Anchovies are the most popular live bait because of their great appeal to a wide variety of game fish, and also because of their relative abundance. Commercial fishing interests, which catch and reduce anchovies to fish meal, have noted this healthy population of anchovies, too, and have pushed for higher commercial quotas for the past several years. No other species of fish has evoked such controversy: Sportsmen fight to hold down the commercial industry's anchovy tonnage allotment to protect the resource, and commercials claim the anchovy resource is underused.

Virtually every major game fish found off the Southland feeds to some extent on anchovies. Yellowtail, albacore, tuna, marlin, calico bass, sand bass, halibut, barracuda, bonito, sheephead, white sea bass, black sea bass, a vast array of rockfish—you name it and it probably eats anchovies.

While anchovy schools may extend for 50 or 60 miles offshore, the really catchable amounts are found close inshore. The fish attain a length of about eight or nine inches, but most used in the live bait fleet are less than six inches long. A short-lived fish, the anchovy has a life span of about four years.

Squid is a seasonal bait, not usually available year-round in Southern California, although they are caught in most months of the year. Especially effective for yellowtail, white sea bass, calico bass, large halibut, and sheephead, the squid is a mollusk with a long, tubular body and 10 tentacles (two long, eight short), two winglike fins at its bottom end, and an ink sac that enables it to squirt and cloud the water when agitated or fleeing from its enemy. (They also show an uncanny ability to occasionally hit an unsuspecting fisherman square between the eyes when he grasps one to use as bait.)

Squid are normally caught for live bait by hanging bright light bulbs over the side of a boat and attracting the fish to the surface lights. The closer the squid "float" to the surface, the easier they are to scoop out of the water.

When live squid isn't available and when the game fish are in a good striking mood, fresh dead or frozen squid can be used effectively.

The live squid is a prime offering for yellowtail, white sea bass, and large calico and sand bass. The squid has a streamline body tipped with two winglike fins at one end and a head and tentacles at the other end. When it becomes frightened, the squid can cloud the water with its own ink.

Mackerel used for live bait include the greenback and the Spanish mackerel. Spanish mackerel are smaller than the greenback variety, hence the Spanish will take more types of game fish. Those most prone to mackerel bait are yellowtail, large calico bass and white sea bass, pretty well in that order.

Mackerel may be caught in the nets of live-bait haulers, or sportfishermen may catch them on rod and reel, using multiple, yarn-adorned hooks on dropper leaders called Lucky Joes, baitless rigs, or mackerel snatchers.

Herring and *tomcod* are sometimes called "brown bait," since both species have a brownish cast to their dorsal sides. The local herring reach a length of about 10 inches, while tomcod ranges up to 15 inches. Both types of bait are caught incidentally in nets during anchovy fishing operations.

Many area fishermen do not realize the potential of the herring and tomcod as fish catchers. Indeed, as a bait stealer, the tomcod can become a nuisance and is often disdained by fishermen, but small tomcod used for bait can be quite effective. On days when calico bass and halibut appear to be uninterested in anchovies (after all, they don't bite well everyday), tomcod or herring hooked through the anus and pitched out without a sinker can be devastating on the game fish.

The *Sardine*, once an abundant prime source of live bait for sportfishing, has been virtually wiped out by unchecked commercial fishing of this species; today only a token catch is taken annually. Most sardines taken by the live-bait industry are caught incidentally while fishing for anchovies. The same species that often strike live squid or mackerel will hit a lively sardine bait.

Sardines rarely exceed a foot in length, and most caught today range from five to seven inches long. Bronzed or yellow backed with green spots, the sardine also has a white underside, no scales on its head, and, interestingly, no lateral line.

Perch and *Pompano* are two inshore species that also show up in live bait nets from time to time. They are rarely used as baits; when they are present in live-bait tanks it is usually in very, very low numbers. Never-

The Spanish mackerel is most commonly used as bait with size 1/0 through 4/0 hooks, depending on the size of the bait. Spanish mackerel are good bait for yellowtail, large calico bass, and striped marlin, the last of which calls for the use of 5/0 to 7/0 hooks.

theless, pompano are sometimes an effective bait for yellowtail, when the yellows are refusing other offerings. Small piling perch and shiner perch are deadly on calico bass.

Live-Bait Techniques

When using live bait, always tie the hook directly to the monofilament fishing line. The line is, in effect, one long leader. After tying your hook to the line, snip off the leftover line so that it will not drag in the water or tip off a game fish that something is afoul with your booby-trapped bait.

A lot of live-bait fishing is done on or near the surface of the water, say no deeper than 15 or 20 feet. For this type of fishing, it's usually best to cast just the bait and hook—no sinker—so that your anchovy (or other bait) is allowed maximum freedom to swim naturally and enticingly where the fish are located.

It takes practice to learn to "fly line" (that is, to cast without a sinker) a relatively light live bait with a conventional rod and reel. The motion used is like a lob, slower than when casting with a sinker or an artificial lure. This is why live-bait rods have been designed with flexible, sensitive tip sections to handle such lightweight casting chores.

When feeding on or near the surface, game fish are most commonly taken by letting them run a short distance with the bait, then flipping the reel into gear and striking. It has long been a matter of opinion as to how long to let a calico bass, yellowtail, albacore, or other fish run with a bait before striking.

As a youngster of about 12 years of age, I once made the mistake of asking a wry veteran of the partyboat wars when to set the hook in a yellowtail.

"When the fish's got the hook in its mouth," he retorted, knowing he himself had just hooked another neophyte.

I still swing and miss plenty often these days, but probably hook my share, too. Here's my advice:

Fast-swimming surface fish such as albacore, bluefin tuna, yellowtail, and bonito are some of the easiest to hook. When one of these species strikes, I lightly thumb the reel spool to prevent a backlash, begin a mental count of one–two–three–four–five, then strike hard. Usually that five-second count is sufficient to allow the fish to swallow the bait.

When using live squid for yellowtail, I increase the count to maybe seven or eight. When using live mackerel for yellowtail it's a bit trickier; you may have to count to nine or 10 or more. Then if you feel the fish has the bait (detected by a "solid" feeling on the line) you can set the hook— two or three times to make sure.

Calico bass and sand bass can be fished with the reel in gear. I am convinced that a bass sucks in a bait, forms it into a mouth-conforming bundle, and swallows it in a mere second. I've hand-fed enough calico and sand bass in a bait tank to see how quickly they inhale a live anchovy. So I catch many of these species by fishing the anchovy on a tight line, waiting past the first couple of light taps and then setting the hook when the rod tip is pulled down sharply.

Again, you have to wait a little while longer when using live squid for bass, simply because the fish has to swallow a larger bait and this takes more time. Wait for that sharp tug that seems to tighten the whole line and that pulls the rod tip down several inches. Then swing.

Barracuda are a bit touchy to hook consistently. If you swing in a second or two after the strike you stand a chance of missing the fish; if you let the barrie swim eight or 10 seconds before setting the hook you may hook more fish but the hook will also be deeper—so that the line can be more easily bitten in two by the fish. I would say I probably hook *and land* more barracuda by letting them run with the bait for about five seconds.

Black sea bass are fished with large bait—mackerel, whole small bonito, whitefish, or slabs of fish—and I prefer to fish with the reel in gear. Rest the bait right on the bottom or just a couple of feet off the bottom and wait. When a black hits he will usually thump the bait a couple of times, then pull the rod tip down in a slow, powerful manner. Lower the rod tip until it is pointed almost right down the line and then try to tear the black's head off. You have to set the hook hard, and more than just once.

One of the most difficult fish to hook is the halibut—at least the smaller members of the species are. Few other species are more deceptive in their bait attack—picking away, twitching the rod tip, running with the bait, stopping, pulling again, tapping away some more—and then when you finally strike, half the time the halibut has vanished. About all the advice I can offer is to wait until the line feels very solid, as if the halibut is hanging on it. Then lower the rod tip, take the slack out of the line and set. Of course, large halibut are easier to hook. They are more likely to swallow an anchovy or live squid in a single gulp.

Here is another cardinal rule of live bait sportfishing: *Change your bait often.* Many times game fish become finicky in their feeding, selecting only the liveliest baits for a meal, and if your wiggly one doesn't have enough spirit it will be consistently neglected. A fresh, "hot" bait is critical when fishing with anchovies, and that in itself involves about 90 percent of the live-bait fishery. Mackerel, squid, and other larger baits can be fished for longer periods of time without being changed.

When I select an anchovy, I don't squeeze the little fish tightly, but rather cradle it in the palm of my hand to prevent injuring it. I also look for an anchovy that does not have a red nose (caused by bumping against the sides of the bait tank) and that does not feel "dry" to the touch (caused by an excessive loss of scales). Both of these types tend to act too sluggish to interest educated game fish.

For some reason, most anchovies have blue backs, but a minority of the small fish have green backs. And for another unknown reason, the green-back anchovies are usually a friskier, healthier, more frantic bait. Look for a greenback anchovy when selecting a bait—it could prove to be the slight edge you need for a successful day. If the anchovy I select doesn't spurt off immediately from the boat following its splashdown, *I reel in and change the bait*. It is absolutely crucial to use the friskiest bait possible. And it is rare when I soak an anchovy, even one that started off lively, for more than five or six minutes without changing it.

All of this bait-changing may sound like a lot of effort—and it is—but it takes little effort to use a poor bait for long periods and catch nothing.

The Happy Hooker

To be a happy hooker you have to know the proper way to hook your bait. Generally, a squid is fished by using a single hook pinned through its tail. For fly lining (using no sinker) an anchovy, the preferred technique is to hook the bait once through its gill collar, but when a sinker of more than ½ ounce is used, the anchovy should be hooked through its nose. Be careful to hook it far enough forward that the point does not penetrate its brain. For surface fishing, mackerel or sardines can be nose-hooked, but hooking them just forward of the ventral fins or through the anus will make them swim deeper without the use of sinker. Perch and pompano may be ventrally hooked or anally hooked.

The following sketches show some of the more popular hooking techniques:

How to tail hook a live squid.

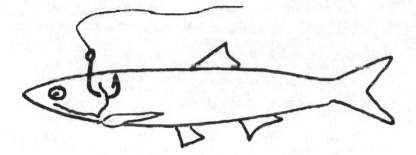

For surface fishing, hook anchovy in gill collar.

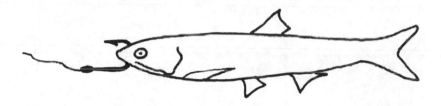

Nose hook an anchovy when using a sinker.

How to hook herring, tomcod, perch through anus.

Which size hook to use for the various baits? The chart appearing below will serve as a *guide*, although actual fishing conditions may call for some exceptions. The *most commonly* used sizes of hooks for the individual baits are in *italics*.

Type of Bait	Hook Size
Anchovy	8, 6, *4*, 2
Squid	1, *1/0*, *2/0*, *3/0*, 4/0, 5/0
Mackerel	
(Greenback)	3/0, 4/0, *5/0*, 6/0
(Spanish)	1/0, *2/0*, *3/0*, 4/0
Herring	1, *1/0*, *2/0*, *3/0*, 4/0
Tomcod	1/0, *2/0*, *3/0*, 4/0
Sardines	1, *1/0*, *2/0*, *3/0*, 4/0
Perch	1, *1/0*, *2/0*, 3/0

4

The Art of Artificial Lures

In Southern California most veteran ocean fishermen use a catchall term—a "jig"—for any and all saltwater lures. Whether it is a spoon, a feather, a candybar shaped lure, or a trolling feather, these collectively are called jigs.

Jig fishing differs from live-bait fishing in several ways. First, most jig fishing gear includes rods with stouter actions and stronger lines, testing most commonly from 30- up to 60-pound test. Second, jig fishing attracts the fisherman who likes to fool his catch with a piece of metal or a bundle of feathers. Third, when fishing is good and the fish are in a mood to readily strike live bait and jigs, the jig fisherman can often outfish the bait fisherman since the heavier jig tackle allows the fish to be brought to the boat sooner. Hence the fisherman gets back in the water to hook another fish sooner, too. Still more time is saved since there is none of the baiting up and rebaiting a hook involved with using a live bait.

However, there are elements of jig fishing to be learned.

I know some jig specialists who have become so engrossed in "throwing the iron" that they *never* fish with live bait; they have, to use the term, become purists. The very best fishermen I know, though, are those flexible enough to learn the proper ways to fish both live bait and jigs, so they can choose the one most effective on any particular day.

Jig Fishing Tackle

Jig-fishing tackle is heavier than comparable live-bait gear for two reasons: (1) jig fishing often calls for casting relatively heavy jigs, which means light lines and soft rod tip actions aren't necessary; and (2) a heavy line tied to a jig seems to spook away fish far less than that same line tied to a hook and live bait. (Probably the fish are so fascinated with the *action* of

51

the jig that they don't notice the line as much.) We are, of course, talking in relative terms; I don't advocate trying to catch bonito after tying 100-pound test mono to your lure.

For a jig rod or rods, I like a medium-action stick, one-piece construction, which may range from 6½ to 8 feet in length. The longer rods in this range would be used when longer casts are necessary. Good jig rods have a heavy butt section to supply sufficient backbone for the power casts in jig fishing. Most jig rods also have a stouter tip section to give more powerful propulsion to the jig; besides, a delicate tip is not necessary to feel a light strike, as it is in bait fishing, because most jig-caught fish hook themselves during the retrieve.

For this type of fishing, lines may range from as light as 15- or 20-pound test to as heavy as 60-pound or more. Those, however, are the extremes. My recommendations for the best all-around line strengths follow:

Fish Sought	Using Small Jigs	Large Jigs
Albacore	25-pound test	40-pound test
Yellowtail	30-pound test	40-pound test
White sea bass	30-pound test	40-pound test
Barracuda	20-pound test	30-pound test
Bass	15-pound test	25-pound test
Bonito	15-pound test	25-pound test

One of the most important qualities of a proper jig fishing reel is that it have a high retrieve-gear ratio. The ratio is determined by how many revolutions the reel spool makes for one revolution of the reel handle. For instance, if a reel has a 2.78 to 1 gear ratio, then for every turn of the reel handle the spool revolves 2.78 times.

The Penn Jigmaster 500 is a good choice for most Southland game fishing for the species listed above. The 500 has a 4 to 1 ratio—relatively high —which allows for fast retrieving of jigs and less arm and wrist fatigue. For heavier jig-fishing work, such as fishing for large game fish off Baja California, the Penn 112H and 113H Senator reels work well, especially when outfitted with the reel components marketed by Newell Manufacturing Corporation, discussed in Chapter 1. The Penn Squidder reel also is a good choice for Southland jig fishing, if the reel is customized with one of the high-ratio transmission boxes (a Powerhouse or a Reel-Deal) that are available at better tackle and sporting goods stores.

Also available for the Jigmaster 500 and the Squidder are Penn accessory handles that allow the angler three choices (three notches) in handle

This barracuda practically inhaled the Straggler jig just barely protruding from its mouth. Barracuda are a great jig fish, often readily striking the artificials when they shun live bait.

length, while also offering a larger handle knob, which I feel better fits the palm of the hand for jig fishing. For many fishermen, the longer accessory handle is more comfortable to use when fast-retrieving jigs.

As a rule, a metal spool is necessary for heavy lines and heavy model jigs and, conversely, using small, lightweight jigs and 15- to 25-pound test usually calls for the ligher weight of a plastic spool or, better yet, a Newellie Spool. A good jig reel should hold *at least* 150 yards of 40-pound test line or its equivalent; many will hold more line.

Types of Jigs

There are many different styles of jigs on the market, including the Salas line of jigs, the Stragglers, Tadys, Spoofers, Hackers, and the bar-shaped Diamond Jig. Whenever you're jig fishing, remember that fish often change their preferences from day to day. What caught fish yesterday, or even an hour ago, may not be effective at this moment. It's best to

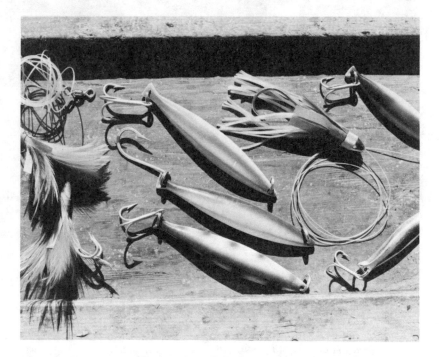

Shown in this photo are five models of Straggler jigs, three at center and two at the far right. Also shown are small bonito trolling feathers. Jigs of the Straggler type come in both lightweight and heavy models, for surface and deepwater jigging, respectively.

This 7-pound bonito was coaxed into striking by a Tady Lure shown here with its manufacturer, Tady Shimizu.

experiment with different types and colors until you discover what they're hitting best. Also having a wide variety of jigs allows you to switch to a particular type if it suddenly starts producing hookups for others on the boat. Watch the other fishermen and see what's working for them.

Briefly, there are four major types of jigs:

Candy-bar Shaped jigs are the most popular today. They have a curved underside, a flat top, and are tapered front and rear (as their name implies, like a candy bar). Examples of this family of jigs includes the Salas, Straggler, Maverick, Hacker, and Jerry Jig.

Wobbler or Spoon type jigs have a concave side and a convex side. Water passing along the sides of the lures give them their kick and they produce a lot of action at even moderately slow speeds. Some of these include the Tady Lure, large Hot Shot Wobbler, the Krocodile, and the Flasher.

A *Hexagonal, Bar-shaped* jig is the Bridgeport Diamond Jig. It is used mainly for deepwater rockfishing, since it is deadly when dropped straight down and yo-yoed up and down a few feet off the bottom.

The *Spoofer* jig is a combination—spoon (at the front) and bar-shaped (at the rear) with a raised waffle design at the end of the jig. The spoon shape gives the jig its action, while the waffle design causes a slight water disturbance and a certain amount of light reflection in the water, to attract the fish.

Some jigs, such as the Tadys, Salas, and Stragglers, come in both heavy and lightweight models. The proficient jig fisherman has a supply of both, since the fish will vary their favorites. While the light jigs normally have more action at a given speed, they do not cast as well or sink as fast as the heavier jigs. On the other hand, the heavy jigs must be retrieved faster (more work for you), and often do not "flutter" or "kick" as much, but they are usually better for deepwater fishing than the light jigs.

Jigs come in a variety of colors and finishes. Some of the spoons and wobblers are available in gold, brass, or chrome finish, but most fishermen use a jig with a painted finish. Among these colors there are some reliable standbys: all white, blue and white, green and white, sardine finish, squid finish, green and yellow, and rainbow finish.

There is actually another class of jigs: Small feathers which are patterned after the original Yankee type jig consisting of a molded lead head section, a long shank hook molded into the head, and a skirt of feathers or plastic strips. A feather differs from the other jigs in that it has no built-in action of its own; the fisherman must make the feather swim, skip, or dance by working the rod tip. One of the most effective retrieves for feathers is holding the rod at about a 45-degree angle, moving the feather back through the water with short, upward twitches of the rod tip, while allowing the feather to sink a foot or so between each twitch. When fish are

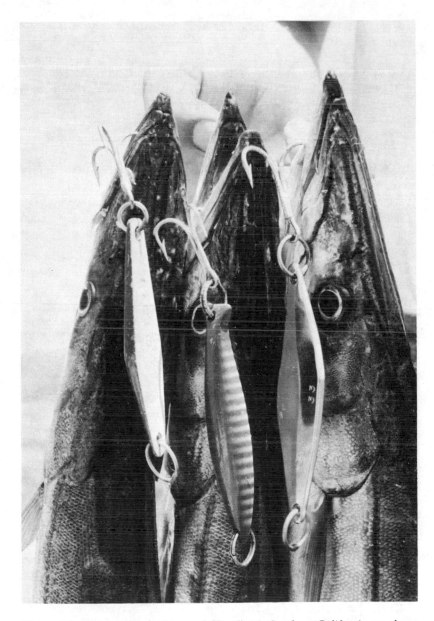

Three of the most popular saltwater fishing jigs in Southern California are shown dangling from the mouths of the barracuda each hooked. From left to right are the Salas jig, Straggler jig, and Tady Lure.

eagerly striking feathers, they can be caught on a *very fast*, straight retrieve.

Years ago, feathers enjoyed wide popularity in barracuda fishing, although they will also catch bonito and calico and sand bass. Today few fishermen use feathers for barracuda, but in the hands of an expert feather man they can still be absolutely devastating on a school of hungry barracuda.

Good feather colors include all white, green and white, green and yellow, blue and white, all black, and all green.

A few years ago some plastic lures originally designed to catch freshwater bass proved very effective on ocean bass, too. Consisting of a lead head and a plastic worm, often with a curly tail or twister tail worm design, these lures include the Scampi, Scoundrel, and Mr. Twister. Sometimes during the early summer bass-spawning season, one of these can be the hottest lure you can tie on your line.

Jig Speeds and Angles

Each jig with a built-in action is designed to look most lifelike at a particular retrieve speed. This means retrieving some lures relatively fast and giving others a slower comeback. You've got to experiment with different speeds to find which one makes a given jig look, in your judgment, most attractive to the fish. At that, the opinion of the fish may sometimes differ from yours and they'll hit the same jig coming fast one day, slow the next.

Usually, the larger and heavier jigs require a fast speed to make them "swim" properly. Here are three retrieve speeds you should keep in mind:

A *very fast* retrieve is *usually* preferred by fast-swimming surface species such as tuna, yellowtail, bonito, and albacore. Actually, it's hard to outrace a speedy game fish with your jig, even at a very fast clip. If they want it, they can catch it.

A *medium-speed* retrieve is often good for calico and sand bass, barracuda, bonito, yellowtail, and white sea bass.

A *very slow* retrieve may do the trick on days when fish refuse the other speeds. Retrieve the jig just barely fast enough to keep it on a proper plane and make it swim. I suspect the reason fish sometimes strike on this retrieve is that it makes them, to use human terms, "nervous" watching that thing move so slowly. Whatever the reason, a very slow retrieve has saved more than one fishing day for me.

You should be familiar not only with the various retrieve speeds but also with the various retrieve angles.

When the fish are on the surface—often evidenced by diving birds or by "boiling" on the surface from fish chasing bait—use a *surface retrieve*.

Cast out, let the jig settle just a few feet, and then start your retrieve so that the jig runs just under the surface. To help keep the jig underwater, lower your rod tip as much as possible, even pushing a few inches of the rod into the water.

If you can detect the direction of surface-swimming fish, such as by observing a series of boils or noticing which way the birds are flying, try to cast a few feet in front of and beyond the fish, so that your jig will intercept them on its return to the rod.

At times the fish will be near the top yet there may be no boils or birds working. The best way to determine this is to watch the other fishermen and note the depth at which they are getting hooked up.

When the fish are down farther—say from about 20 feet to 50 feet—a jig cast retrieved on about a *45-degree angle* may draw the most strikes. When the fish are close to the boat and hungry, the "45" retrieve also works well when preceded by a simple underhand lob cast. Let the jig settle down to the fish level, then begin your retrieve.

The *yo-yo retrieve* involves letting the jig sink straight down alongside the boat. A good choice when deepwater fishing, this retrieve can be accomplished in two ways: the straight yo-yo, or bouncing the jig. In the straight yo-yo, the jig is simply dropped to the bottom, then retrieved rapidly straight up to the surface. You should be alert to a possible strike, however, as the jig is sinking. In bouncing, the jig is raised sharply off the bottom, then allowed to settle and flutter back down; this is done by raising the rod tip from about an 8 o'clock position to an 11 o'clock position, then quickly dropping it back to 8 o'clock. The sharp pull on the jig with a tight line causes the lure to flutter. The action roughly resembles that of a live squid swimming.

You can also *pump a jig* along just below the surface. At times this is a good retrieve for yellowtail and surface-feeding white sea bass. Cast out with a lightweight jig, allow the lure to settle a few feet, raise the rod tip to shoot the jig forward, quickly drop the rod tip to let it flutter, take up the slack, and repeat.

5

Troll, Troll, Troll Your Boat

Most Southern California offshore fishing is done from an anchored boat, less frequently from a drifting boat, and sometimes even while trolling from a moving boat.

One of the biggest advantages to trolling is that dragging lures behind a boat allows you to search out a lot of territory in a limited time. The disadvantages include the fact that not many people can fit comfortably in the

Noted fisherman Charley Davis holds binoculars to scan the surface of the water for signs of fish. Sometimes fish can be seen flashing or boiling on top, or birds may be seen hovering or diving into baitfish that game fish are feeding upon.

stern of a boat at one time, so the number of people who can participate is limited. This may not be a problem on a smaller private boat or charter boat, which does not carry many passengers anyway, but consider that out of 50 people on a partyboat, only half a dozen may be able to troll at any time.

While there are a multitude of different fish off the coast, today only a few species really respond well to the troller. All are migratory fish that move seasonally up and down the coast—the bonito, albacore, and striped marlin.

Evidence of surface schools of any of these fish are diving or circling birds following the fish, jumping fish or boils on the surface, or fish rippling the surface or "flashing" just underneath the water.

Whenever you approach a visible school you should always troll so that just the outer fringes of the school come within range of the jigs. Moving into the center of the school will most likely spook the fish and send them sounding for the bottom.

If the boat you are trolling aboard isn't equipped with rod holders, a vest harness and rod-butt belt will help immensely to hold your fishing outfit and prevent unnecessary fatigue.

Always be sure your reel drag is properly set when trolling. A drag set too tight may rip the hooks out of the fish's mouth when it strikes or, worse yet, it may break the line. Conversely, a drag that is too loose may not set the barbs deeply enough to hook and hold the fish.

Trolling for Bonito

At certain times of the year huge schools of bonito may swim offshore waters during their migrations up and down the Southland coast. Usually ranging from two pounds to about six pounds—although much larger bonito to nearly 15 pounds are taken occasionally—the bonito may pass as close as a few hundred yards offshore or as far as several miles offshore.

Since bonito are not particularly large fish, regular live-bait fishing outfits and 20- to 30-pound test lines can be used to troll for them. The most popular lures are the chrome-headed bonito feathers, or small albacore feathers, from four to six inches long. Blue and white, red and white, all white, and all black are good color choices.

Most bonito are taken between trolling speeds of five and eight knots. The feathers should be towed astern no more than 75 feet away. If your feather skips out of the water too much at your desired trolling speed, you may have to hold your rod tip down so that the line cuts through the water at a lower angle.

The bullet-headed trolling feather manufactured by Straggler jigs is a good bet for large bonito or smaller albacore. Note double hook used to rig this lure.

Trolling for Albacore

If there is one species that will readily hit a trolled jig, it is the albacore. Appearing off the coast about late June each year and often staying within range of fishermen well into the fall, the albacore schools are actually *located* by the sportfishing fleet trolling each day to determine where, or if, the fish have moved from their previous location.

Albacore trolling requires somewhat heavier gear than trolling for bonito. A 4/0-size reel (a 113H Penn is good) packed with 50-pound test line is a good choice, although some fishermen like the insurance of a 6/0 reel and 60- or 80-pound test line. Most albacore caught off the Southland weigh under 40 pounds, but the heavy gear is used to quickly bring a hooked longfin in to the boat. Many veteran ocean fishermen believe that a hooked albacore will often be followed by the school for a while, and that if the hooked fish is quickly landed the school will swim near the boat.

As soon as a trolling hookup occurs, live bait should be chummed (tossed) over the side in the hope of further attracting the longfin school. Once the school is near the boat, continually light chumming can hold it there for some time while live bait is used to catch more fish.

Many longfin fishermen make the mistake of trolling too far back, thus eliminating the possibility of bringing the school in quickly once a hookup occurs. At no time should the jigs be more than 100 feet behind the boat, and more often they should be pulled no more than 60 to 75 feet behind the vessel.

Albacore trolling feathers can be purchased at most Southern California tackle shops, partyboat landings, and sporting goods stores. Most of these feathers have circular heads (although the Fenwick Hex Head jigs have a hexagonal form) and are cone shaped; either feathers or a plastic skirt trails behind the head and at least partially hides the 4/0- to 8/0-size hook. The fishing line is passed through a hole in the tip of the head of the lure, the lure is threaded up the line, and then the hook is tied on to the end of the monofilament. When pulled through the water, the lure rides back against the eye of the hook.

Sometimes rigging two, three, or four of these feathers in tandem on the same line will bring more strikes than a single feather. This tends to be more effective on larger albacore, however, and not so much with fish under the 20-pound class.

Fenwick Hexhead trolling jigs are excellent attractors for albacore, the long finned migratory tuna. These lures use a colored plastic skirt rather than feathers.

If you're fishing aboard a private boat and you arrive on the albacore grounds, it's usually best to work the area with a general zig-zag course. This doesn't mean zigging for 60 seconds and zagging for 60 more, though, as you would be constantly maneuvering the boat. Run at one angle for 10 or 15 minutes, then change the angle for 10 or 15 minutes, so that you have long zigs and zags. Once you find a good fishing area, it often pays to circle that spot after every hookup period. The fish may be feeding in that one location and not moving much at all.

Trolling for Striped Marlin

Because a very small percentage of ocean sportfishermen troll for striped marlin each year, it will not be covered here in any great detail.

Marlin trolling usually calls for a 4/0-size reel loaded with 30- or 40-pound test line, or a 6/0-size (114H) holding 50- or 80-pound test. Big-game trolling rods are used, usually with a roller-type tip guide and some-times with a gimbal butt that allows the end of the rod to be fastened to a fighting chair. The most popular trolling lures are the psychedelic-colored

Anglers search offshore waters for marlin, trolling from their center-console-model cruiser. Note outrigger poles mounted just in front of console.

Photo by Al Tetzlaff

*Trolling for marlin can quickly erase several hours of no action when a hookup
finally occurs and a sight like this breaks water. Tiny fish attached to marlin's side
is a parasitic remora.*

feathers measuring about 10 to 12 inches and containing a single, Siwash
style hook ranging in size from 7/0 to 10/0.

When flying fish are used as trolling bait, the flyers are far more effectively trolled from boat outriggers, which keep the lines high and out from
the boat, thereby making the flyers skip enticingly across the surface at the
proper trolling speed. Sometimes marlin are taken by trolling close to
sighted fish; at other times blind strikes occur when a hidden subsurface
fish suddenly rises and strikes the jig or bait.

Since marlin fishing usually entails using the boat to chase the hooked
fish, and since few people can troll at one time and a single hookup may
require a half hour to several hours to land, partyboats rarely, if ever, are
used to troll for marlin. Most private boats aren't equipped for marlin
fishing, either. Most marlin fishermen own a boat large enough to be slip
berthed and to fish open blue water.

6

The World of Partyboating

In the ocean fisherman's vocabulary, "partyboat" doesn't mean a vessel on which a celebration is being held, although on a few trips some of my fellow passengers seemed more interested in partying than fishing. An open partyboat (called head boats on the Gulf and East coasts) makes regularly scheduled runs to the fishing grounds, and tickets for a fishing space are sold to the *individual*. Charter boats, on the other hand, are rented in their entirety. There is one flat fee for the use of the boat and an entire group charters the boat and pays this fee, no matter how many or few persons are in the group.

As examples, a partyboat with a 50-passenger limit might charge $25 per person for a day of fishing. Even if only 20 passengers go fishing, the cost remains $25 each and the boat earns $500 for the day, instead of a possible $1250. A charter boat capable of carrying 50 passengers might charter for $850 a day, so if 20 passengers charter the craft they, in effect, still collectively pay $850.

The advantages of chartering a boat are that the group can usually decide where they will fish; and of course the group chooses its own members. On an open partyboat the skipper chooses the location and you have no control over who else is fishing on the boat.

There are about 30 sportfishing landings along the Southern California coast, stretching from Morro Bay in the north to Imperial Beach, below San Diego, in the south. Most of these facilities offer both open partyboats and charter boats, as well as parking areas, tackle shops, tackle rental, cafes or restaurants, and other services. Statewide, some 850,000 passengers ride licensed partyboats and charter boats each year, about 650,000 of them in Southern California alone.

All boats have live-bait tanks, galleys, and fish-cleaning services available. In addition, many have bunk areas for sleeping and some of the most

A passenger who buys a ticket aboard a partyboat also, in essence, hires the services of a guide. The partyboat skipper uses his experience and expertise to select the most likely good fishing spots.

modern craft even have lounges, sun decks, and showers for passenger comfort. The types of trips offered from the sportfishing landings are diverse:

Half-day fishing trips usually last about five hours and fishing begins within an hour or so of the departure point. Most landings offer at least two half-day trips daily—one in the morning and one in the afternoon. The morning trips usually depart sometime between 5 and 8 a.m.; the afternoon trips between noon and 2 p.m.

Normally no sleeping facilities are offered on half-day jaunts, since the fishing time is relatively short. Virtually all half-day boats do offer galley services, however.

Three-quarter-day trips are actually expanded versions of the half-day trips. On these trips you can fish a little farther from port and usually stay out two to three hours longer. These trips usually leave between 5 and 7 a.m. and return between 2 and 3 p.m.

No bunks are available, but a hot galley is offered.

All-day island or freelance trips attract the most serious fishermen, simply because on these trips you may fish areas 50 or more miles distant and consequently obtain better results from less heavily fished waters. All-day trips usually leave between 12 midnight and 3 a.m., returning from 3 p.m. to 6 p.m., depending on the distance traveled and the fortunes of the day. Sometimes, if the fish prove uncooperative, the skipper will stay out longer to give anglers a longer opportunity for a successful catch.

All-day trips have bunks available, but the cost of using them is not included in the partyboat ticket. Fishing gets underway early in the morning, often just about daybreak. The boat usually begins its trip back to port between noon and 2 p.m.

Sundown or twilight trips are operated by some landings during the summertime when daylight savings time is in effect and the water is warm, for then fish like calico bass, sand bass, bonito, and barracuda feed well in the early evening.

Most sundown or twilight trips depart between 5 and 6 p.m. and fish for about five hours in local waters. Many people who work during the day fish on these trips at night.

Albacore fishing trips are the longest one-day trips. The migratory longfins often are situated 60 to 100 miles offshore, which necessitates an early departure and late return for the boat. Some individual albacore trips may last up to 20 hours or more, departing between 10 p.m. and midnight and returning between 6 p.m. and 10 p.m. The time spent fishing is also dependent on the whims of the fish—some trips return much earlier when the fishing is good.

Albacore trips, of course, have both bunk accommodations and full galley service.

Considered a nuisance by most ocean anglers, a Pacific blue shark is gaffed from aboard a partyboat off the Southern California coast.

The black sea bass, which grows to weights in excess of 550 pounds, was caught more frequently in the early days of Southern California sportfishing. Today the blacks are fewer in number locally, but some long-range trips to Baja California still take good catches of this heavyweight bottom fish.

Bottomfishing trips are featured heavily in winter, when water temperatures cool and most game fish either migrate out of the area or virtually quit biting. The bottomfishing cruises—operated as half-day, ¾-day and all day trips—concentrate on rockfish such as salmon grouper, red snapper, chilipeppers, chuckleheads, cowcod, and lingcod. Heavy gear is needed here, since multi-hook leaders are used to depths ranging from 250 feet to nearly 700 feet.

Partyboat Practices

There are certain practices common to partyboating. First, it's always best to make an advance reservation for your trip, even if you suspect the boat will be lightly loaded and obtaining a space will be no problem. At least by making a reservation you let the sportfishing landing know to expect you at a certain time (always leave your phone number so you can be reached should a trip be cancelled). Of course, during the peak of the

Some partyboat operations include a fish-cleaning service in the price of a ticket: in this case a tip is suggested. In other cases the crew charges separately for cleaning fish.

The most exotic and exciting type of trip offered by Southland sportfishing landings is the multi-day, long-range trip leaving from San Diego ports and fishing off Baja California. Here part of a big catch is being unloaded from the Qualifier 105, *a 105-foot all-aluminum deluxe craft.*

season many other fishermen ride partyboats and it may be necessary to make your reservation(s) several days in advance, especially for weekends.

Should you find you cannot keep your reservation commitment, by all means contact the landing and cancel your reservation. Don't become a "no show" and tie up a space another eager fisherman could have used.

Many boat crews give each passenger a rotation and sack tag that tears in half, one half being attached to your fish sack and the other half to be carried by you to verify you are fishing in the proper spot at any given time. Normally, passengers are rotated at regular intervals so that each group of people gets a chance to fish at all the stations around the boat. Rotations move clockwise along the rail.

You may bring your own fish sack aboard the boat (those large burlap potato sacks serve nicely) or buy one for a nominal price at the landing or aboard the boat. Most landings also rent both surface-fishing and bottom-fishing rod and reel outfits, and also sell terminal gear.

Prices for bunks range from $3 to $5, depending on the landings and the boat involved. Galley menus normally include such dishes as bacon and eggs, ham and eggs, hamburgers, ham sandwiches, cheese sandwiches, beer, soda pop, and milk.

Many boats have rod racks lining the sides of the superstructure, so that anglers can store their rods and reels during a trip. In addition, the crew will clean your catch, sometimes at no extra charge (although a tip is usually anticipated) and sometimes at an extra charge, depending on how the skipper operates his boat.

A Guide to Partyboat Landings

Following is a list of Southern California partyboat landing operations, ranging from Morro Bay in the north, to Imperial Beach in the south. Most landings operate both daily half-day trips and all-day trips. In addition, many landings feature tackle shops, restaurants or cafes, charter boats bookings, tackle rental, and other services. All can provide you with current fishing information for their respective areas.

Listed geographically, from north to south, these operations include:

MORRO BAY
  Virg's Landing
  1215 Embarcadero
  (805) 722-2216

  Brebe's
  1001 Front Street
  (805) 772-2788

AVILA BEACH
  Port San Luis Sportfishing
  Pier 3
  (805) 595-7200

GOLETA
  Goleta Sportfishing
  Goleta Pier
  (805) 967-2104

SANTA BARBARA
  Sea Landing
  Santa Barbara Breakwater
  (805) 963-3564

VENTURA
  Ventura Sportfishing
  1500 Anchors Way
  (805) 644-7363

OXNARD
  CISCO Sportfishing
  3825 Pelican Way
  (805) 985-8511

PORT HUENEME
  American Sportfishing
  Foot of Harbor Street
  (805) 488-2212

PARADISE COVE
  Paradise Cove Sportfishing
  28128 W. Pacific Coast Hwy.
  (213) 457-2511

MALIBU
  Malibu Pier Sportfishing
  23000 W. Pacific Coast Hwy.
  (213) 456-8030

SANTA MONICA
  Santa Monica Sportfishing
  Municipal Pier
  (213) 395-4230

REDONDO BEACH
Redondo Sportfishing
181 N. Harbor Drive
(213) 372-3566

SAN PEDRO
Ports O'Call Sportfishing
Berth 79
(213) 547-9916

22nd Street Landing
141 W. 22nd Street
(213) 832-8304

LONG BEACH
Queen's Wharf
555 N. Pico
Berth 53-54
(213) 432-8993

Belmont Sportfishing
Foot of 39th Place
(213) 434-6781

SEAL BEACH
Seal Beach Sportfishing
Foot of Main Street
(213) 431-1374

NEWPORT HARBOR
Art's Landing
403 Edgewater
(714) 675-0550

Davey's Locker
400 Main Street
(714) 673-1434

DANA HARBOR
Dana Wharf Sportfishing
25152 Del Prado
(714) 831-1850

OCEANSIDE
Oceanside Sportfishing
314 Harbor Drive South
(714) 722-2133

MISSION BAY
Seaforth Landing
1717 Quivera Road
(714) 224-3383

Islandia Sportfishing
1551 Mission Bay Drive
(714) 222-1165

SAN DIEGO
Fisherman's Landing
2838 Garrison Street
(714) 222-0391

Point Loma Sportfishing
1403 Scott Street
(714) 223-1627

H & M Landing
2803 Emerson
(714) 222-1144

Palm's Long Range Sportfishers
Foot of Emerson Street
(714) 224-3857

7

Fishing Aboard Private Boats

An estimated one million ocean fishermen a year angle from private boats in Southern California offshore waters. Their craft range in size from tiny skiffs to super deluxe blue-water sportfishers, and range in price from under $1000 to tens of thousands of dollars.

Fishing from a private boat is a much more personal and intimate way of fishing, for there are relatively few people aboard, all of them usually know each other (or soon do after the trip begins), and the boat itself is usually much smaller and closer to the water than a large partyboat or charter boat.

The fact that a boat is relatively small, however, does not mean it cannot be well equipped for offshore fishing. Of course, you're not going to be able to cram in a lot of fishing gear and appointments in a 12-foot dinghy, but boats in the 18- to 22-foot class can now be purchased or outfitted with virtually all of the equipment carried by the larger sportfishing cruisers. There are, I believe, several qualities that make a private boat a real fishing machine. How many of these features does your boat contain?

A live bait tank that holds at least three scoops of anchovies.

Rod racks to hold fishing rods out of the way when not in use.

A tackle storage compartment to hold coiled leaders, feathers, jigs, extra reels, line, and other gear.

A flying bridge or tuna tower to place the operator high enough to spot distant surface fish.

Outrigger poles for marlin trolling.

A fathometer to show water depth and fish habitat structure (a line-marker type is preferred to the "flasher" unit).

A trio of offshore fishermen troll in search of marlin. Though small, this seaworthy boat features a tuna tower from which to spot fish on the surface, outrigger poles, and twin outboard power for added reliability and safety far from shore.

A fish storage area to stow the catch and keep it fresh.

Twin engines for added reliability and safety.

Easy access to the bow, in case you have to follow a fish completely around the boat.

Rod holders, to eliminate the strain of hand-holding fishing outfits for long periods of trolling.

A fighting chair (if you're after marlin or swordfish).

Some sort of wind and spray protection in rough weather.

Adequate fuel capacity to make extended trips to the more distant fishing grounds.

A *reliable* compass.

An emergency signalling kit.

A large-capacity bilge pump.

A tackle-preparation or bait-cutting board.

A small gaff and a landing net for smaller species of fish; a flying gaff in case a real monster is hooked.

Good Manners Afloat

When fishing from a private boat, there are some rules of courtesy to other boaters to be observed. One of the most frequently committed discourtesies is passing or anchoring too close to other boats.

Few things upset a partyboat skipper more, for instance, than to have an unthinking private boater come speeding in close to the partyboat when a school of fish is being chummed and held close to the larger vessel. The predictable result is usually that the school of fish is scattered and driven off and no one—private boat anglers and partyboaters alike—catches anything. Nearly as bad is anchoring so close to a partyboat or another private boat that fish are needlessly lost by tangling in the anchor lines or in the lines of fishermen on the other boat.

When boats bunch too close together, all the maneuvering and motor noise often sends the fish away and no one enjoys success. Even if the fish remain, many hookups are lost on the anchor lines and fishermens' lines of nearby boats.

Floating kelp paddies sometimes attract yellowtail and albacore offshore. Small baitfish, seeking the shelter of the paddy, attract the larger game fish. During warm water cycles, dolphin can be taken from under paddies in waters offshore from San Diego.

Another practice to avoid is attempting to troll through a fleet of boats when the rest of the vessels are at anchor. This will only serve to put down any fish in the area or to tangle lines and raise tempers.

Actually, the best anchor position in relation to a partyboat is about *75 to 100 yards downcurrent.* Usually, the current will be running from the bow to the stern of an anchored boat (although the current occasionally will run "uphill," against the swell); therefore, anchoring 75 to 100 yards (not feet) off the stern of a large partyboat is a good spot. Why? Because the partyboat carries a large load of anchovies that are chummed, and once in the water the anchovies swim downcurrent and often the best fishing is found just out of casting range of most of the partyboat fishermen—and right where you can anchor without interfering with their fishing.

Sometimes yellowtail will be found offshore holding under small, floating kelp paddies. Many private boaters practice paddy hopping—moving from paddy to paddy—dropping baits and casting jigs next to the kelp to see if any yellows are home. Once a small bunch of fish is found, that particular paddy may only be large enough to support one private fishing boat. Yet a few boat operators become so brash that they will charge up to a small paddy already being fished and cut in on the action.

Most of the private boats used for marlin fishing are large enough to slip berth in a marina and are capable of fishing farther out on the blue water grounds.

Light Tackle Fishing

One of the fun things about fishing aboard private boats is that much lighter tackle can be used since there are far fewer lines to become tangled with and close friends are less likely to get irritated if one particular fish takes a long time to land. Fishing from private boats, I've caught a 22-pound yellowtail on 6-pound test line, a 24-pound roosterfish (off Baja California) on 6-pound test line and a 14-pound albacore on only 4-pound test line. In all probability I couldn't have caught any of those fish on such light gear on a 50-passenger ticket boat.

Even if you hook a very large fish that would otherwise be capable of stripping off all your line, a private boat can be used to chase the fish and retain a certain amount of line on the reel spool. That procedure is seldom followed aboard partyboats.

Whenever you have a school of fish around a private boat, make sure someone takes the responsibility to occasionally toss a little chum in the water to hold the fish. If everyone is hooked up at once and they become captivated with the great fun they're having, chumming may be accidentally overlooked and the school will slip away.

8

A List of the Nine Most Wanted

In this chapter we deal briefly with nine of the most significant species caught by Southern California offshore fishermen. To select nine species out of the nearly 550 different fish that fin off the Southland coast is indeed being arbitrary. But for their fighting characteristics, their quality as table fare, and their availability and popularity, I think most knowledgeable ocean anglers in the region would agree that these nine are the most appropriate choices.

Some of the nine species are extremely popular with sportfishermen (for instance, albacore), yet are present only a few months of the year; others are particularly exciting to catch (striped marlin), but are far fewer in number than such abundant types as calico and sand bass. Still others (rockfish) do not produce a particularly sporting fight when hooked, but have been included because they are the mainstay of winter fishing and are considered excellent food dishes.

In 1968 the California Department of Fish and Game conducted a survey of Southern California partyboat skippers, asking them to "list in order the 20 most important species of fish to *your* partyboat business." From their answers a popularity list was compiled. Eight of the species described in this chapter ranked as the top 8 choices of partyboat skippers; only the striped marlin that I have included here did not appear on the "top 20 list"—obviously, since partyboat operations rarely if ever include marlin fishing in their trips.

The results of the 1968 partyboat skipper survey were:

Ranking	Species
1	Barracuda
2	Bass (calico and sand)

3	Yellowtail
4	Bonito
5	Halibut
6	Rockfish (included bocaccio)
7	Albacore
8	White sea bass
9	Bluefin tuna
10	Sculpin
11	Pacific mackerel
12	Black sea bass
13	Sheephead
14	Lingcod
15	Jack mackerel
16	Salmon
17	Cabezon
18	Miscellaneous flatfish
19	Sablefish
20	White croaker

No doubt, since 1968, some of the top-ranked fish have changed positions for varying reasons. For instance, significantly fewer barracuda are now taken since the imposition of a 28-inch minimum-length limit a few years ago. As a result, if a new survey were taken, the calico and sand bass would most probably be ranked number one today. Similarly, a 22-inch minimum-length limit on halibut has been imposed since the survey. And because fishermen are currently allowed only one white sea bass under 28 inches, juggling has most likely taken place with these fish. Still, I feel that the 1968 survey reflects accurately the top-ranked *group* of nine fish today.

Albacore

The Southern California albacore season traditionally begins in late June or early July and extends through early October (although sometimes lasting into late November). Early-season fish are generally smaller—from 8 to 12 pounds. But the longfins grow as the season progresses; late-season fish commonly average 25 to 30 pounds, and some topping 40 pounds are not uncommon.

During recent years the albacore migration pattern has shifted so that two major sportfishing centers have developed—one off San Diego and the other off the Morro and Avila bays area. Off the latter location the longfins generally swing closer into shore, where a run of only 15 to 30 miles may

The albacore is a football-shaped bundle of muscle that usually visits local offshore waters from late June or early July through early fall. Most albacore caught here range from 12 to 20 pounds, although late-season fish approaching 40 pounds are not uncommon.

be necessary to reach the fish. Off San Diego, Oceanside, Newport Beach, San Pedro, and Oxnard runs from 60 to 100 miles may be necessary to reach the fish. These distances are flexible, though. In "good" albacore years the fish will swing closer to shore and in "poor" runs they will be farther from shore, when only the very fringe of the huge schools is reachable by day boats.

Albacore fishing differs from most other forms of fishing in that once a school is brought close, all fishing is done from a drifting boat in very deep offshore water. The depth eliminates the chance that hooked fish will tangle your line in kelp, rocks, or an anchor line. Still, plenty of fish are hooked and lost because of tangles with other fishermen.

When a school of particularly hungry fish is found, the longfins will hit a dead bait. Also, if a dead bait is dropped over the side and dragged through the water as the boat is drifting to a stop following a trolling hookup, albacore will frequently hit it. The wise albacore fisherman is constantly at the rail of the boat, alert to the first signal of a trolling strike, so that he can get a bait in the water fast. At times only the first few baits will be struck by a fast flurry of fish and then no more hookups occur.

A medium-action live-bait rod and 20-pound test line is a good starting point for live-bait albacore fishing. If fishing gets "hot" you can switch to heavier line—up to 40- or even 50-pound test in the best action. A size 4 or 2 hook are good choices when using anchovies.

Yellowtail

Yellowtail fishing is usually best in the late spring, and sometimes again in the fall, although in some years good catches have been taken virtually year-round in certain areas. By far the area consistently best for yellows is the Coronado Islands, located 18 miles south of Point Loma, San Diego, and in Mexican waters. During the peak of the season, catches of over 200 yellowtail per partyboat or charter boat are not unusual.

Other significant catches of yellowtail can occur at San Clemente Island, Catalina Island, the La Jolla kelp area, off Rocky Point and San Onofre (off the Orange County coast), and under floating kelp paddies offshore.

Live squid, when available, is a prime bait for yellows. Since a lot of the fishing takes place near islands, over reefs, and next to kelp beds, some hooked fish are lost by tangling in the kelp or cutting the line on the rocks. When fishing near these hazards, you should put the maximum pressure possible on a hooked yellowtail—short of breaking the line—so that the fish is stopped before escaping.

Yellowtail can become extremely touchy feeders, so on days when the fish can be sighted but are not hitting well, it's good strategy to drop down to using 15- or even 12-pound test line and small hooks.

Like the albacore, the first run of a hooked yellow can be a long, fast, powerful surge, during which some fishermen panic and tighten their drag, forget to hold their rod tip high, or clamp a thumb on the reel spool to stop the fish. That, of course, is usually a bad mistake. A reel-drag mechanism is a much more sophisticated and objective braking device than a thumb.

Most yellowtail taken off Southern California range from 10 to 20 pounds in weight, although yellows exceeding 40 pounds are not rare. Off Baja California, the long-range sportfishing trips sometimes bring back yellowtail exceeding 60 pounds.

White Sea Bass

This largest member of the croaker family found off Southern California is a highly prized catch. It is a good fighter, is relatively scarce in number, and is one of the finest-tasting game fish to be caught.

Few places produce enough white sea bass today to be considered their "prime" fishing grounds, but some significant catches are usually taken each winter near the Coronado Islands, below San Diego, where the fish move in following schools of spawning squid. Other flurries of white sea bass action can occur at Catalina Island, Santa Cruz Island, and at Carpinteria, near Santa Barbara. Lesser numbers of the fish are taken all along the coast, from shallow inshore waters and bays to the outer islands.

Many consider live squid the top bait for white sea bass. At one time, sportfishermen using squid clusters (two or more squid hanging on a very large treble hook) took a high percentage of the fish, but in recent years a single squid pinned on a single 2/0 to 4/0 hook seems to produce best.

The white sea bass has a relatively soft mouth, and care should be taken not to overwork a hookup, or else a large hole may be ripped in the fish's mouth and the hook can slip out at the slightest hint of slack line. Whites brought up from deeper water will often burst their air bladders, causing them to float near the surface and giving the appearance of a huge tongue sticking out of their mouths.

Whites in the 12- to 25-pound class are the most commonly caught, but some trophies exceeding 70 pounds have been taken in recent years.

In a really hot white sea bass bite, especially when a school of the fish is drawn up from the bottom, they can be readily taken on jigs. A light-colored jig seems to work best on most occasions, with all-white the old standby choice. Sometimes the sea bass will strike at a very slow retrieve and at other times they like a jig sinking straight down, then yo-yoed up and down off the bottom.

The white sea bass—actually not a bass at all, but a member of the croaker family —is a prized catch off Southern California. This fisherman had exceptional success in landing a trio of 30-pound class whites on one trip.

Barracuda, Bass, and Bonito

For most Southland ocean fishermen the "three Bs" are the staples of the near-shore surface fishery. None of these species achieves the size of the albacore, white sea bass, or yellowtail and, to put it bluntly, can often be caught by fishermen with less experience and expertise. Don't mis understand, however; any of the "three Bs" can turn quite finicky and quickly separate the skilled anglers from the unskilled, too.

Barracuda, bass, and bonito can be caught in virtually any month of the year—at least somewhere—but the best fishing occurs when water temperatures reach 60 or 62 degrees in the spring and then continue warm through the early fall. All three fish are common and may be taken all along the Southland coast and the outer banks and islands.

Live-bait fishing accounts for most of the catch, and the fish are often attracted to the surface, where flylining a bait is most effective. In addition, all three are good jig fish, readily hitting artificial lures when hungry. The barracuda, bass, and bonito are grand sport on light spinning tackle and some aficionados of the long wand specialize in using fly fishing equipment on private boats, or boats chartered expressly for that purpose. One of the best fly fishing areas for bonito, by the way, is inside of King Harbor, Redondo Beach, where a warm-water outlet from an electrical generating plant keeps the water temperature ideal for most months of the year.

The curly-tail and twister-tail types of lead head plastic worms have proved to be the most devastating lures on sand and calico bass in the last few years. During the "hottest" fishing periods, usually in late spring or early summer, when the bass spawn, the rate of action with these lures is often a fish a cast. Another excellent bass attractor is a lead head with a small live squid, fresh dead squid, or a strip of squid attached to the hook. Many strikes occur as the jig is sinking.

The calico and sand bass combined represent the single largest annual catch of surface game fish taken by Southlanders. In a top fishing year, well over a million bass will be caught. There is a 12-inch minimum-length limit on the species.

Barracuda are notorious line nippers, and fishermen once used wire leaders between hook and fishing line to prevent cut lines. Today, however, *many more* barracuda are hooked by monofilament line tied *directly* to hooks than by the use of wire leaders, since the fish have become keen-eyed. The barracuda is an extremely slimy fish, and you'll be looking for something to wipe your hands with after handling just one barrie.

Pound-for-pound, bonito are perhaps the hardest-fighting fish that is caught in this region. I shudder to think what a 300-pound bonito would fight like, if they grew that large. A 10-pound bonito is all most fishermen can handle on light tackle, although the majority of the catch is under 6 pounds.

Barracuda most commonly weigh between 3 and 4 pounds in the sport catch, although 8- to 12-pound "logs" were much more common up to the late 1950s. Calico bass are most often taken in the 2- to 4-pound class, but they can reach as high as 12 pounds and over.

Halibut

The halibut is one of the strangest-looking fish taken by sportfishermen. It is a flatfish, with both eyes on one side. Its upper side (which faces the surface of the water) is a tan to dark brown, to help hide it from its enemies above, as the halibut lies on a sandy bottom. Its bottom side is white, so that, when swimming, it is barely discernible from a vantage point below it.

Most halibut are taken in relatively shallow water—from a maximum of 60 feet all the way into the surfline. Many trips operated specifically for halibut fish waters from 40 to 15 feet deep.

These "flatties" inhabit virtually the entire coast of Southern California. In good fishing years, many halibut are taken in the flats area between the Coronado Islands and the Mexican mainland; in upper Santa Monica Bay, between Topanga and Santa Monica Canyon; at Catalina Island, off the Channel Islands area, Santa Rosa Flats, and Goleta and Carpinteria.

A particularly spectacular run of very large halibut usually develops for a few weeks each late spring at Santa Rosa Flats, when sportfishing boats from Oxnard, Port Hueneme, Santa Barbara, and Ventura run up catches as high as 100 per boat. Moving into the area to spawn, the halibut there range from a *low* of about 20 pounds to a high exceeding 50 pounds.

An anchovy drifted along sandy bottom and coupled to a shiny chrome torpedo sinker about 30 inches up from the hook is a good inshore halibut rig for the smaller fish. However, most of the "barndoors" of the Santa Rosa Flats run are taken on live squid and correspondingly larger hooks.

As mentioned in an earlier chapter, halibut can be particularly difficult to hook, except for the large ones which tend to quickly gulp a bait.

Since the halibut is a flat-shaped fish, it is important that you hold the fish as near to a horizontal position as possible for it to be gaffed; otherwise sinking the gaff hook into the fish can be difficult.

Like barracuda, halibut are very slimy; wipe your hands after handling one or you'll probably have trouble gripping your equipment.

Most halibut caught by sportfishermen weigh from 4 to 10 pounds. The peak season ranges from spring through early summer, with minor peaks in late fall.

Rockfish

Over 50 varieties of rockfish are taken off the Southland, principally during the winter months when water temperatures have cooled and surface game fish have either been hit by a case of lockjaw or have evacuated south to warmer climes.

Of the deeper rockfish, the lingcod (to 50 pounds) and the cowcod (to 40 pounds) are perhaps the two most prized. These two species can be taken on jigs, and fishermen using very heavy lures in deep water take a good share by yo-yoing the jigs up and down off the bottom.

Most rockfish, however, are caught while bait fishing—with live or dead anchovies, live or dead squid, or slabs of other fish—and fishermen use multihook ganion rigs. Rockfishing isn't exactly the epitome of sportfishing, either, since large reels, heavy lines, stout rods, and heavy sinkers are used. A lot of bottomfishermen like a 6/0-size reel, 80-pound test line, and a rod little short of a broomstick action. The reason for the heavy equipment becomes more evident when you consider it's often necessary to dredge up several fish (which collectively could weigh 30 to 60 pounds) at one time, plus a three-pound sinker and 700 feet of line.

Bottomfishermen put up with such work because rockfish are delicious table fare—and during the winter it's usually the only game in town.

By far the most plentiful rockfish is the salmon grouper or "bocaccio," the backbone of the shallow-water bottom fishery. It usually weighs from 1 to 3 pounds, while lingcod average about 10 to 15 pounds and cowcod 8 to 12 pounds. Other commonly caught rockfish include the red snapper (not a true snapper), the chilipepper, chucklehead, barberpole, bolina, bank perch, and, in shallower waters, the sculpin.

Virtually every sportfishing landing posts some rockfish in its daily fish counts—more heavily in the winter than the rest of the year. Some of the prime rockfishing grounds include the Morro Bay and Avila Beach regions, the Channel Islands, Volcanic Reef and South Bank in Santa Monica Bay, Catalina Island, San Clemente Island, Tanner Banks, and the Coronado Islands.

Currently there is a liberal 15-fish daily limit on rockfish, including cowcod, but up to 5 lingcod per day may be added to that figure, allowing a total of 20 fish. The regulations also allow sportfishing vessels to operate multiday rockfishing trips, on which the legal limit applies per passenger per fishing day.

Striped Marlin

The striped marlin is one of the glamour species, a fish that can be a spectacular leaper when hooked and can reach weights locally in excess of

Photo by Al Tetzlaff

One of the glamour species of the Southland is the striped marlin, named for vertical stripes along its side, which show prominently in the fish pictured.

200 pounds. A few marlin are taken incidentally each year aboard party-boats and commercial charter boats, usually when the fish hit albacore feathers being trolled on the longfin grounds, but the vast majority of the take indicates that the striped marlin is a private-boat fish.

Most of the time the marlin fishing season really gets underway in late August and can continue through early November. September and October are the peak months.

Marlin are taken principally on trolled psychedelic feather jigs or on live bait—usually a Spanish mackerel, but less frequently greenback mackerel will work. There is nothing quite as exciting as seeing the tailfin of a surface-swimming marlin standing erect, then cutting an agitated, staccato swath toward the live bait you just cast or slow-trolled near the fish. The marlin has the unique trait of "lighting up" like a neon light, radiating an iridescent blue when it becomes excited.

Fishermen out after striped marlin once used relatively heavy gear, but with the refinement of tackle the trend during the past 15 years has been to light tackle. Some billfishermen now prefer catching marlin on 4/0- and

3/0-size reels and 20- and 30-pound test lines, rather than just killing another fish on 80-pound test.

The marlin has an extremely tough mouth, and when one strikes a trolled feather (or a flying fish towed by outriggers) the boat operator usually applies throttle to use a short burst of boat speed to help sink the hook. When fishing from a drifting boat and using live bait, it's a good idea to signal the skipper when you're ready to strike, so he can shoot the boat forward to help set the hooks.

There are several sportfishing, yacht, and marlin clubs in the Southland —the Balboa Angling Club, Avalon Tuna Club, and Marlin Club of San Diego, to name but a few—and these groups hold a series of marlin fishing tournaments throughout the course of the season. Some of the events encourage tagging and releasing marlin, so that a later recapture of the fish will aid scientific investigations of the species' growth and migration habits.

9

From Watery Realm to Table

Catching a fish is only the first of a four-step process that results in a tasty morsel for your mouth. Besides catching, you've got to keep your catch fresh, clean it, then cook it.

Some fish are needlessly wasted each year, chiefly because the angler did not keep them cool enough to slow the spoilage of bacteria growth. Generally, stowing your catch in a wet burlap bag will be sufficient to keep it fresh for a fishing day, but the sack cannot be allowed to completely dry out in hot weather. It takes only a few seconds to toss a couple of buckets of water on the sack or to dip it in the ocean. A wet burlap sack creates coolness by evaporation.

Of course, an ice chest filled with chipped, flaked, or cubed ice will keep your catch in better condition if it is practical to take such a unit along on your trip (which usually cannot be done on partyboats, with their limited space).

Cleaning Your Catch

The catch should be at least gutted at the end of your fishing while the boat is returning to port. Gutting is easy: Simply insert the tip of your knife just below the anus of the fish and slit open the stomach to a point just between the ventral fins. Reach into the slit and pull out all the innards in the body cavity. At this point you may also want to cut off the fish's head (cut just behind the two pectoral fins), although I prefer to leave heads on if I'm going to fillet or skin the fish later.

When you're ready to complete the cleaning process (many fishermen do this after arriving home) you have your choice of two basic methods: either filleting or cleaning the fish without removing its bones.

A burlap sack, such as those used for shipping, is a fine way to store your catch during a day of fishing. Keeping the sack wet will keep your catch cool by the process of evaporation.

The proper care, cleaning, and cooking of your catch are the three steps necessary to most fully use what comes home in your fish sack. This catch of mixed barracuda, bass, and mackerel is about to be gutted on a private boat fish-cleaning board.

If you wish to leave the main body of the fish intact, say for baking, first scale your fish (a commercial fish scaler is good, as is the edge of a knife or even the tines of a dinner fork). Because the scales overlap each other in the direction of the tail, they are dislodged as you move your scaling instrument from the tail toward the head. For best scaling results, rake back and forth, with more downward pressure as you move toward the head.

After scaling, cut the fish's head off and remove all of its fins by running the knifepoint along each side of the fin base, then pulling the fins free. Then cut off the tail. Your fish is now ready for baking whole or steaking into several crosswise pieces.

Some people like to skin their catch. This is best accomplished by leaving the head on the fish until after the skinning is completed. Cut through the fish on both sides just behind its head, taking care *not* to cut through the backbone. In this way you can grasp the head for a firm hold while skinning. Now cut around the base of all fins and remove them. Then insert the knifepoint under the skin at the upper head end of the fish and, working carefully, separate the skin from the meat until you have enough skin loosened so that the piece can be gripped with a pair of pliers. Hold the head of the fish firmly in one hand, grasp the flap of loosened skin with the jaws of the pliers and pull slowly and evenly toward the tail. Repeat the process on the other side of fish.

Filleting a fish is very easy, although some fishermen think there's a culinary magic to it. Filleting is actually faster than the other methods and it leaves the leftovers virtually all in one big piece.

To fillet, grasp the fish by the head and, if the knife is in your right hand, lay the fish crosswise in front of you with its tail pointing to the right; reverse if you are left-handed. Begin by cutting down through the fish in back of its head at a point just behind its pectoral fin. Stop cutting when you feel the knife hit the backbone and turn the knife edge toward the tail so that you can slice all the way down the backbone. While slicing, angle the knife edge *very slightly* downward, so that you stay in contact with the backbone all during the cut. Continue slicing until the knife cuts through the outer skin of the fish at the base of its tail. You now have one complete slab cut from the side of the fish.

Flip the slab over so that it is skinside down on your cleaning board. Cut out the rib cage (which can be easily seen at this point) to eliminate bones.

To skin the slab, slice slowly through the meat at the very tip of its tail section, taking care *not* to cut all the way through the skin. Turn the blade away from you and, using slow slicing motions, run it back and forth between the inside of the skin and the meat. To aid in this operation, pull the tail end of the slab toward you slowly as you slice and separate.

After cleaning, your catch should be rinsed with fresh water, but use just enough so that the pieces are clean. Over-rinsing tends to take away some of the flavor. Immediately after rinsing use paper towels to pat dry your pieces.

And into the Pan

(The following ocean fish recipes are supplied courtesy of Karen Green and Betty Black, coauthors of *How to Cook His Goose (and Other Wild Games)*, New York: Winchester Press, 1973.)

Barbequed Albacore Steaks

4 albacore steaks,
½-inch thick

½ cup melted butter

½ cup fresh lemon juice

3 tablespoons sherry or
vermouth (optional)

There are a lot of tuna sandwiches here, or a lot of barbequed albacore steaks, depending on how you prepare the catch. It's easy to see how albacore got the nickname of "longfins"—note the very long pectoral fins on these fish.

Wash steaks and, using a paper towel, pat dry. Combine butter with lemon juice; combine sherry with vermouth if used. Using this baste, brush both sides of fish. Steaks should be barbequed about 7 minutes on each side, while basting frequently. When ready, fish should flake easily when touched with a fork. Serving portion: 4

Italian Barracuda

4 barracuda steaks, about ¾-inch thick	1 cup Italian salad dressing contains oil, vinegar, basil, garlic, salt, pepper)

Use salad dressing to marinate fish steaks for 2 to 4 hours in refrigerator. Punch holes in a piece of aluminum foil and use foil to cover barbeque grill. Fish should be barbequed on foil for 8 to 10 minutes, basting frequently. Turn fish once on grill during barbequing. Serving portion: 4

Halibut Ahoy

4 halibut steaks, about ½-inch thick	4 slices sandwich cheese (round cheddar or American)
Salt and pepper	2 cups milk

Place halibut in single layer baking dish. Sprinkle with salt and pepper and top with cheese slices. Pour milk on top of fish, so that fish is nearly covered. Bake for 30 minutes in 350-degree oven or until fish flakes easily when prodded with a fork. Serving portion: 4

Tropical Baked Lingcod

4 lingcod fillets, about 8 ounces each	1 grapefruit
½ lemon	Dash of tabasco
1 cup light white wine (chablis)	2 sprigs cilantro (if unavailable, watercress may be substituted)

Rub lemon over the fillets and set aside. Peel the grapefruit and remove all membrane; then cut into ⅛-inch thick slices, cutting each slice further into 4 wedges. Pour wine into bottom of casserole, then place fillets on top of fruit. Sprinkle with dash of tabasco sauce. Next place in layer of small, hand-torn cilantro leaves. Top with remaining grapefruit wedges and pour remaining wine over top. Bake in 350-degree oven for 18 minutes, or until fish flakes. Serving portion: 4

Baked Snapper

½ lemon

1 teaspoon garlic powder

1 teaspoon lemon-pepper marinade

4 strips bacon

4 8-ounce red snapper fillets

1 teaspoon dried parsley flakes

Rub cut lemon on fillets, then sprinkle both sides of fish with lemon-pepper, garlic powder, and dried parsley. Wrap each piece in waxed paper and keep refrigerated until cooking time. Use a greased casserole dish and place fillets in and top with bacon. Bake fish at 350 degrees for approximately 20 minutes. Test doneness with a fork. After cooking is completed, discard bacon. Serving portion: 4

Bass in Baskets

4 ocean bass fillets, about 8 ounces each

½ pound mushrooms, sliced and sauteéd

1 cup sour cream

½ lemon

2 tablespoons melted butter

½ pound small seedless green grapes

½ cup mayonnaise

Salt and pepper

Paprika

Combine sour cream, butter, mayonnaise, grapes, and mushrooms, then add a squeeze of lemon juice. Spoon mixture over each fillet and bake for 20 minutes in 350-degree oven, or until fish flakes. To brown fillets slightly, broil for 1 minute. Sprinkle with paprika and serve in foil baskets. Serving portion: 4

Skillet Sea Bass

2 pounds ocean bass fillet

10¼-ounce can marinara sauce

1 onion, diced in large chunks

3 large pitted black olives, sliced

1 green pepper, cut into large pieces

1 tablespoon commercial chili sauce

4 tablespoons cooking oil

1 tomato, cut into wedges

¼ teaspoon each: salt, pepper, garlic powder

½ cup dry Sauterne wine

Pour oil into large, heavy skillet and add salt, pepper, and garlic powder. Slowly sauté onion and green pepper until soft, but not dark. Combine chili sauce with marinara sauce in small bowl, then add to ingredients in skillet. Add wine and stir. Place fish in skillet and add tomato and olives. Spoon sauce mixture entirely over fish, cover skillet, and cook over low heat for 20 minutes. Remove lid and cook additionally until fish flakes easily when touched with a fork. Serving portion: 4 to 6

10

It's Called A What? . . .

No wonder beginning ocean fishermen can become confused over the identification of the different types of fish that inhabit Southern California waters. Hundreds of varieties swim here. In its "Guide to the Coastal Marine Fishes of California," the California Department of Fish and Game describes no less than 554 individual species, which fall within 144 families of fish.

To attempt to identify that many species would, of course, involve an entire book in itself—and one larger than this. So presented here are sketches and a brief description of 13 of the most popular and commonly caught species. Learning these types alone will enable you to identify the vast majority of fish you'll catch off the Southland.

Also presented with each species is a length, weight, and age-comparison chart, to give you some idea of the growth patterns of each type of fish.

Albacore

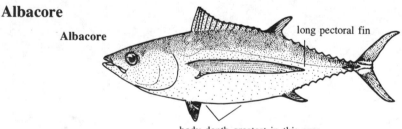

Albacore

long pectoral fin

body depth greatest in this area

The albacore is found worldwide in warm seas. In the eastern Pacific the fish (a member of the tuna family) ranges from Guadalupe Island to Southeastern Alaska. The largest documented catch in the world weighed

93 pounds and was about 5 feet long, but off Southern California a 50-pounder is considered a trophy. The albacore is dark gray to blue-black above its lateral line, silver gray below. Perhaps its most distinguishing feature is its elongated pectoral fins, giving it the nickname "longfin."

Length	Weight	Age
21 inches	7 pounds	1 year
25 inches	12 pounds	2 years
30 inches	20 pounds	3 years
34 inches	30 pounds	4 years
37 inches	37 pounds	5 years
39 inches	48 pounds	6 years
41 inches	54 pounds	7 years

Barracuda

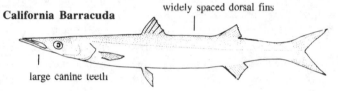

California Barracuda

widely spaced dorsal fins

large canine teeth

Extending from the extreme ranges of Cape San Lucas, Baja California, to Kodiak Island, Alaska, the Pacific barracuda has been reported to be 5 feet long, but more recent California records indicate the fish grows to 4 feet and about 18 pounds. Barracuda are usually taken at depths ranging from the surface down to 80 feet. The fish, slender in shape, are sometimes called "logs" (large specimens) or "pencils" (small ones). Barracuda have a pointed snout and a wide space between the two sets of dorsal fins. They sport a mouthful of large canine teeth and are known for their line-cutting ability. The barracuda is dark brown with bluish reflections above its lateral line, silvery below. They are an extremely slimy fish.

Length	Weight	Age
14 inches	6 ounces	1 year
20 inches	1 pound	2 years
24 inches	2 pounds	3 years

30 inches	4 pounds	5 years
35 inches	6 pounds	7 years
38 inches	7 pounds	9 years

Barred Surfperch

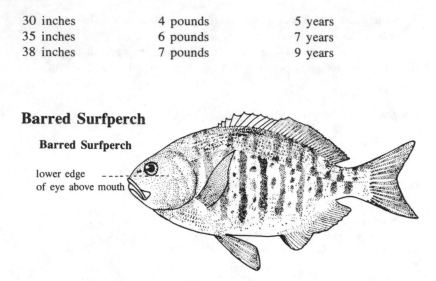

Barred Surfperch

lower edge
of eye above mouth

The barred surfperch has been found from Playa Maria Bay, Baja California, to Bodega Bay, California. The barred perch has reached lengths of 17 inches and weights to 4½ pounds. One way to distinguish barred perch from other types of surfperches is that the lower edge of the eye of the barred variety stops above a line drawn back from the upper edge of the mouth. The barred surfperch, common off California, is olive-green to yellow-green on its back, silvery below, with vertical bars on its sides.

Length	Weight	Age (Females)
5 inches	1 ounce	1 year
7 inches	3 ounces	2 years
10 inches	10 ounces	3 years
12 inches	1 pound	4 years
14 inches	2 pounds	6 years
16 inches	3 pounds	10 years

Bocaccio

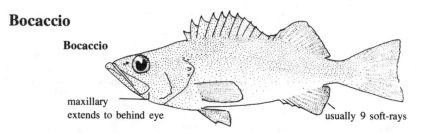

Bocaccio

maxillary
extends to behind eye

usually 9 soft-rays

The bocaccio, or salmon grouper as it is commonly called by local fishermen, is a rockfish taken in depths ranging from shallow water down to nearly 1000 feet. It has been documented from Point Blanca, Baja California, to Kruzof and Kodiak Islands, Alaska. Extremely common off Southern California, often dominating the catch in certain areas, the bocaccio is uniform dusky-red on its back, pinkish below. Young of the species have dark brown spotting on their sides.

Length	Weight	Age
7 inches	1 ounce	1 year
10 inches	6 ounces	2 years
16 inches	1½ pounds	4 years
23 inches	5 pounds	8 years
26 inches	7 pounds	11 years
30 inches	11 pounds	17 years

Corbina

California Corbina

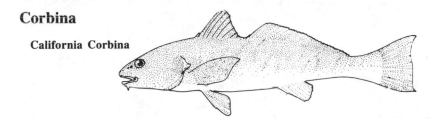

The California corbina has been recorded from the Gulf of California to Point Conception, California. Corbina are a surf fish, although they have been caught in water as deep as 40 feet. The body is a uniform gray with incandescent reflections and wavy diagonal lines on its sides. A member of the croaker family, the corbina has a barbel under its lower jaw that is believed to be part of its olfactory system and an aid in locating food.

Length	Weight	Age
4 inches	½ ounce	1 year
10 inches	5 ounces	2 years
13 inches	12 ounces	3 years
15 inches	1¼ pounds	4 years
17 inches	2 pounds	5 years
18 inches	2¼ pounds	6 years
20 inches	3 pounds	8 years

Halibut

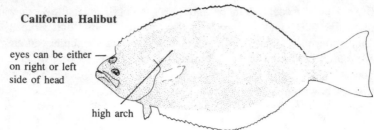

California Halibut

eyes can be either — on right or left side of head

high arch

Reaching a length of 5 feet and a weight of 72 pounds, the California halibut is a relatively slow-growing fish. It has been noted in the Gulf of California and from Magdalena Bay, Baja California, to the Quillayute River, British Columbia. The halibut's upper side ranges from a medium brown to almost a deep black, while its underside, which lies on the bottom, is white. Since halibut are a broad flat fish, large specimens are sometimes called "barndoors." California halibut have been caught from the surface to as deep as 300 feet, although they are most commonly taken from 10 to 60 feet.

Length	Weight	Age (Females)
10 inches	6 ounces	1 year
14 inches	1 pound	2 years
19 inches	2½ pounds	3 years
27 inches	7 pounds	5 years
38 inches	22 pounds	9 years
45 inches	36 pounds	13 years
49 inches	46 pounds	18 years

Kelp Bass

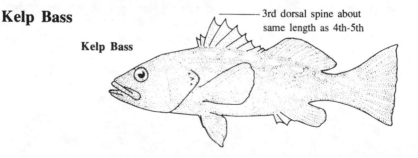

Kelp Bass

3rd dorsal spine about same length as 4th-5th

The kelp, or calico bass, is a true sea bass with a slow growth pattern. In California, commercial fishermen are not allowed to catch kelp bass or its relative the sand bass. Kelp bass are found from Magdalena Bay, Baja California, to the Columbia River. Although they can weigh nearly 20 pounds, fish over 12 pounds are considered rare. Taken from the surface down to about 150 feet, the kelp bass is characterized by an olive or brown coloring with whitish angular blotches and spotting on its back.

Length	Weight	Age
4 inches	½ ounce	1 year
5 inches	¾ ounce	2 years
9 inches	5 ounces	4 years
12 inches	13 ounces	6 years
16 inches	2 pounds	10 years
18 inches	3 pounds	12 years
19 inches	3½ pounds	14 years
20 inches	4¼ pounds	16 years

Opaleye Perch

Opaleye

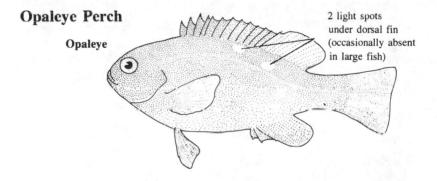

2 light spots
under dorsal fin
(occasionally absent
in large fish)

The opaleye perch, which derives its name from the brilliant opalescent blue-green color of its eye, ranges from Cape San Lucas, Baja California, to San Francisco. Fish to 25 inches and nearly 13½ pounds have been observed, but catches in excess of 5 pounds are noteworthy. Opaleye occur most commonly in the intertidal zone. Their color is a dark olive-green, usually with two light spots at the base of their dorsal fins. Since the California Department of Fish and Game has just recently begun intensively studying the opaleye, no data on age are yet available.

Length	Weight
6 inches	2 ounces
10 inches	11 ounces

13 inches	1½ pounds
16 inches	3 pounds
20 inches	6 pounds
24 inches	10 pounds
25 inches	11 pounds

Pacific Bonito

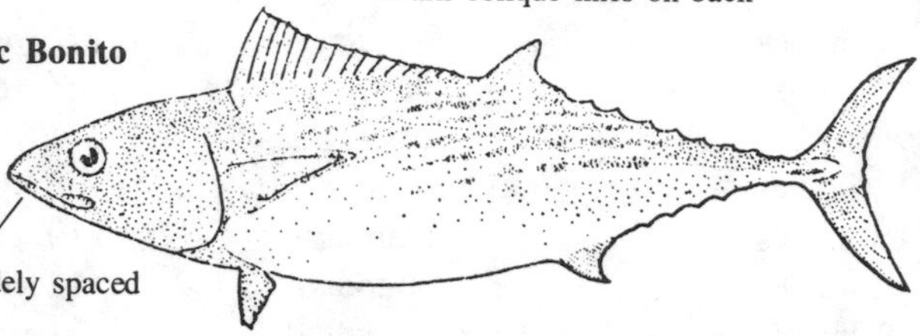

Dark oblique lines on back

Pacific Bonito

teeth large, usually widely spaced

Found from Chile to the Gulf of Alaska, the Pacific bonito is a member of the mackerel family (not the tuna family; indeed, all tunas are actually members of the mackerel family) and reaches a weight of over 20 pounds, although fish over 15 pounds are relatively scarce. Off Southern California, the bonito is found in greatest abundance from Santa Monica Bay to points south. Bonito are dark blue-black above, silvery below. The species is also characterized by dark parallel lines running obliquely along its back and by large, usually widely spaced, teeth.

Length	Weight	Age
19 inches	2¼ pounds	1 year
25 inches	6 pounds	2 years
29 inches	10 pounds	3 years
30 inches	11 pounds	4 years
31 inches	12 pounds	5 years
32 inches	13 pounds	6 years

Pacific Mackerel

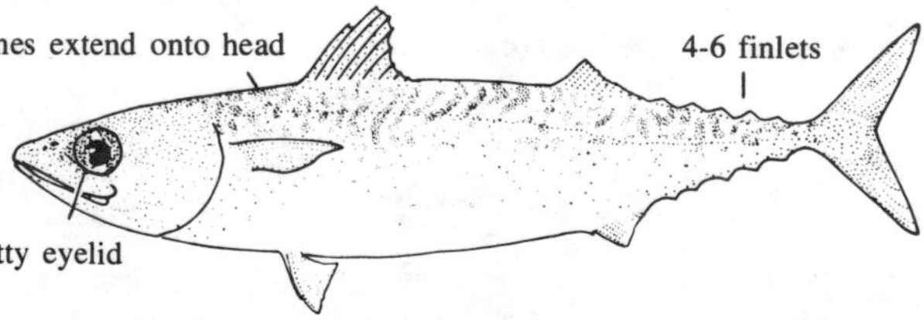

wavy lines extend onto head

4-6 finlets

Pacific Mackerel

eye with fatty eyelid

A trans-Pacific species, the Pacific mackerel is found in the eastern Pacific from Chile to the Gulf of Alaska. It has a dark head, a back characterized by dark wavy lines and is silver-green on its sides and underside. In a survey of some 23,000 Pacific mackerel, at least one fish was determined to be over 11 years old. The Pacific mackerel also has 4 to 6 finlets between the second dorsal and anal fins and its tail. Over the eye is a fatty eyelid.

Length	Weight	Age
11 inches	10 ounces	1 year
12 inches	13 ounces	2 years
14 inches	1½ pounds	4 years
15 inches	2 pounds	6 years
16 inches	2½ pounds	8 years

White Croaker

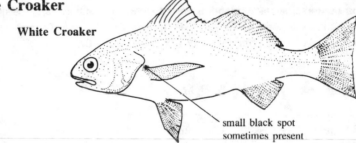

White Croaker

small black spot
sometimes present

Also called tomcod or kingfish, the white croaker is probably the fish most commonly caught from Southern California piers. At this writing, complete age data for the white croaker are not available. Present from Magdalena Bay, Baja California, to Vancouver Island, British Columbia, the white croaker is identified by its incandescent brownish to yellowish coloring on its back, with silver coloring below and fins yellow to white. A small black spot is sometimes present near the base of the pectoral fins. The fish is somewhat blunt in shape and has an arching lateral line.

Length	Weight
4 inches	½ ounce
8 inches	3 ounces
10 inches	6 ounces

12 inches	11 ounces
14 inches	1 pound
15 inches	1¼ pounds

White Sea Bass

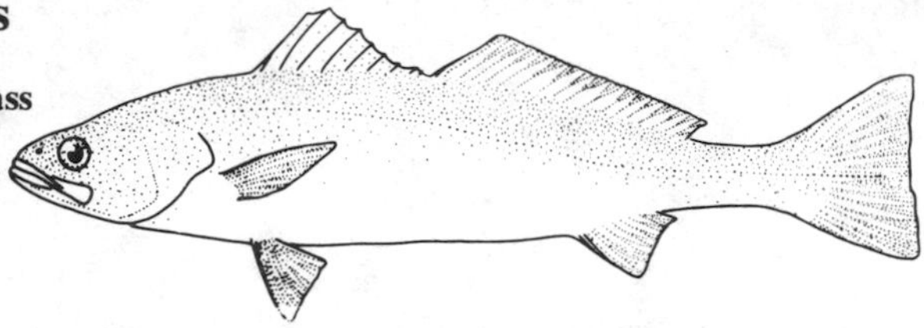

White Sea Bass

row of small teeth –
in roof of mouth

The white sea bass is not a member of the bass family at all, but is actually a member of the croakers. An isolated population is found in the upper Gulf of California, while in the Pacific the "white" stretches from Magdalena Bay, Baja California, to Juneau, Alaska. The heaviest record-ed weight of the species to date was 83 pounds. The fish is bluish to gray on its dorsal surface, blending into a silvery color below. Dark speckling sometimes appears on its back and upper sides. Young of the species have several dark bars running vertically along the sides.

Length	Weight	Age
8 inches	3 ounces	1 year
14 inches	1 pound	2 years
20 inches	2½ pounds	3 years
32 inches	11 pounds	6 years
38 inches	18 pounds	8 years
46 inches	31 pounds	12 years
48 inches	35 pounds	14 years
50 inches	40 pounds	16 years

Yellowtail

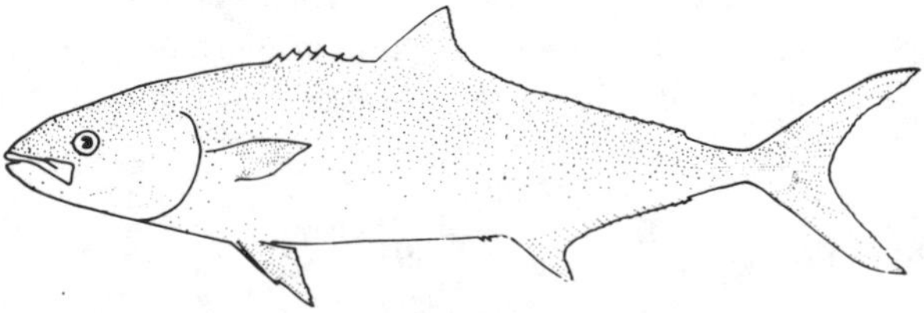

Yellowtail

Yellowtail reach weights of over 80 pounds, although those most commonly taken off Southern California weigh from 10 to 20 pounds.

This member of the jack family is found in the eastern Pacific from Chile to southern Washington, though seldom in any significant numbers north of Point Conception, California. The yellowtail is olive-brown to blue above, has a muted yellow stripe running horizontally along its side, and has yellowish fins and tail. It is a streamlined fish, mistaken by many fishermen as a species of tuna.

Length	Weight	Age
18 inches	2 pounds	1 year
25 inches	4½ pounds	2 years
33 inches	11 pounds	4 years
43 inches	23 pounds	8 years
47 inches	31 pounds	10 years
49 inches	33 pounds	12 years

11

A Potpourri of Fishing Tips

Always back off the star drags on conventional reels and the turnknob drag adjustment on spinning reels when the reels aren't in use. This will prevent the drag washers from sticking together and will also relieve unnecessary tension on the drag mechanism, giving it longer life.

You can produce additional drag on a fighting fish by using the thumb of your left hand (on a conventional reel) and laying it over the line, holding the line down against the foregrip of the rod. This is best achieved during the lifting phase when pumping on a hooked fish.

Always rig up all of your fishing outfits while traveling to the fishing grounds. The very best fishing may occur as soon as the boat stops.

To see at a glance what pounds test line your reels contain, attach to the sideplate of each reel a small piece of white adhesive tape on which the number has been written with a felt-tip marker.

When bottomfishing with live mackerel bait use your diagonal pliers (or a knife) to clip off about two-thirds of the length of each section of tail fin. This will allow the mackerel to remain lively, yet not so frisky that it drags your hook and sinker across the bottom.

Let out the "fishing length" of monofilament line and drag it behind the boat for a few minutes while traveling to the fishing grounds. Don't attach anything to the end of the line; let the drag of the water pull the line from the freespooled reel. This procedure will let you check the line for any frayed spots, it will get the line wet so that it lays smoothly on the reel spool, and it will reveal any underwraps that may have snarled the line.

If you're not certain your hooks are razor sharp, pull the hook point smoothly across your thumb nail. With only the lightest pressure, the hook point should dig in slightly.

To check for any invisible wear that has occurred inside rod guides, run a piece of women's hosiery through the guide. The fabric will snag at the slightest surface irregularity.

Watch the "hot corner" of the boat for fish boiling (feeding) on the surface. This is the spot on a partyboat where the deckhand throws the chum.

Throw away any hooks that show the slightest sign of rusting. If you try to economize by saving them, they may infect the other, good hooks in the same box.

When you place your rods in a rod rack, arrange them in order from the lightest to the heaviest. That way you can locate a given type of outfit in a hurry.

Shiner or piling perch, plus herring, are highly effective yet little-known baits for calico and sand bass.

Live-bait fishing for halibut? Try using a chrome-plated torpedo sinker instead of the dull gray rubbercore sinker. Halibut seem to be attracted to shiny objects, and the chrome weight will help lure the fish to your bait.

Insert your hook into the anal area of your bait, if you want the bait to swim downward without using a sinker.

To mark a fish you caught for later identification, use a pair of diagonal cutters to fin clip your catch. You may, for instance, clip off the tip of one tail fin and one pectoral fin as your own personal "brand." It has settled more than one argument.

One of the handiest and most effective ways to keep fish fresh during a day of fishing is to put them in a burlap sack. Keep the sack wet and the resulting evaporation will keep the catch cool.

A short section of single-strand wire used directly in front of a saltwater jig will sometimes make the lure "kick" more and improve its fish appeal. The wire should test from 50 to 80 pounds and be used in a 30-inch section.

Fishing rods can be carried neatly together in a bundle by using rubber-bands to hold the rods together. Bunch the rods together, slip one end of a rubberband over a guide and then stretch the band for several turns around the rods, looping the remaining end over another guide. Repeat the process in about four places along the length of the rods.

When your fish is clearly visible under the surface of the water, yell "Color!" This will alert the deckhand or your fishing partner that a gaff will be needed soon.

On extended fishing trips, never leave leather rod-butt belts or vest harnesses out overnight. Nighttime moisture will soak the leather and you'll be faced with a wet mess in the morning.

Tuck away a large plastic trashcan liner in your tackle box. Should the weather get sloppy, the bag can be used to cover your tackle box, preventing a lot of tackle trouble.

Worn fishing rod guides or tiptops can fray line and lose you fish, but often neglected are worn swivels, snaps, split rings, and sinker-ring eyes. Be sure to check these items, too.

When you rinse off your rods and reels with fresh water after a trip, don't forget to also rinse any jigs you may have used. Lures are subject to the same corrosion that attacks rods and reels.

Periodically spray the exposed hardware on your tackle box with aerosol lubricant. You'll add years to the life of box components.

A roll of plastic electrical tape should be in every tackle box. If a rod guide comes loose, the tape can be used to hold it in place. The tape will also hold a reel onto a rod in an emergency.

Special Section:

A GUIDE TO BAJA LONG-RANGE AND RESORT FISHING

Baja California juts conspicuously into its saltwater sheath for a distance of over nine hundred miles, its slender, leg-shaped form suggesting how millions of years ago it broke from the continent. To the west, the rugged peninsula is touched by the Pacific Ocean; to the east, by the fish-rich Sea of Cortez.

It is a country where *manana* is truly good enough; where civilization has, to a large degree, not advanced into the mainstream of the twentieth century; where yuccas and saguaros dot the landscape and cattle meander across highways. Materially, most of the people are poor, but they are rich in life. They own treasures rare to the U.S.—unhurried days, star-splotched nights, unspoiled air, pristine oceans, clean, sandy beaches. Along with this romanticism of yesterland is a charisma created by some of the finest big-game fishing in the world.

The Sea of Cortez has been called a natural fish trap. This is not a heavily-exaggerated statement. Warm water currents sweep along the submarine ridges and reefs paralleling the Baja peninsula, carrying with them an abundance of tiny marine organisms. These, in turn, attract the smaller forage fish which, in their role as ingredients of the food chain, lure in the flamboyant exotics—the billfish, dorado, yellowfin tuna, wahoo and roosterfish considered by many veteran deep-sea anglers to make up the most sought after species in our regional waters.

Anglers are attracted for many reasons to these exotic species. For the marlin angler, the thrill of watching a twisting, jumping, tail-kicking and greyhounding striped marlin put on a spectacular acrobatic exhibit no doubt supplies much of the charisma. The broadbill swordfish fancier faces the challenge of making one of the wariest fish in the sea take a bait and, once a swordfish is hooked, the battle can continue for hours.

113

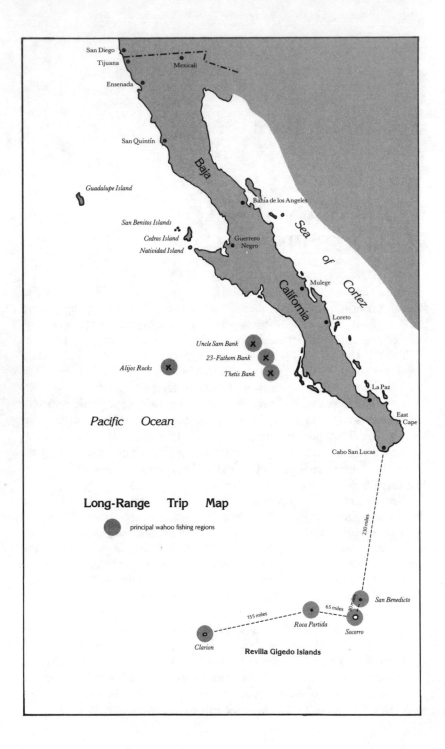

San Diego
Tijuana
Mexicali
Ensenada

San Quintín

Baja

Guadalupe Island

Bahía de los Angeles

San Benitos Islands
Cedros Island
Guerrero
Negro
Natividad Island

Sea

Mulege

of

California

Loreto

Cortez

Uncle Sam Bank
23-Fathom Bank
Alijos Rocks
Thetis Bank

La Paz

East
Cape

Pacific   Ocean

Cabo San Lucas

Long-Range   Trip   Map

principal wahoo fishing regions

230 miles

San Benedicto

155 miles

65 miles

Roca Partida

Socorro

Clarion

Revilla Gigedo Islands

The unfurled dorsal of a sailfish is a unique feature of a species that seldom exceeds 130 pounds, but on light tackle—and some anglers use very light lines on spinning, baitcasting and fly rod gear—the sail is a grand leaper, often jumping right next to the boat. Like the sailfish and striped marlin, large blue and black marlin can take to the air, and fishermen often hope they will, for the energy expended while jumping more quickly tires these fish. Otherwise, a huge blue or black marlin may fight for 10, 12, 14 or more hours before the fish is landed . . . or it breaks away to freedom.

Wahoo are fish of the fast lane—spectacular streakers and wild strikers —even if the fight is often short-lived. The dorado, a high-wire aerialist, is a beautifully-colored species which puts up a spirited struggle on light tackle and represents one of the most delicious varieties ever placed on a dinner plate.

Second perhaps only to the broadbill in stamina, the yellowfin tuna is a blood-and-guts, slug-it-out adversary that fights all the way to the boat. And on light tackle, the roosterfish is considered by many anglers to be faster than the albacore, more determined than the yellowtail, and grand sport in shallow water, where the roosters can sometimes be stalked like tarpon or bonefish on a Bermuda flat.

How does one get to Baja, to do battle with some of the most exciting game fish in the world?

If you own your own boat, and it's large enough (and you're wealthy enough to support it), you can cruise it down the Pacific side of Baja, to Cabo San Lucas, and enjoy pursuing billfish, dorado, wahoo, roosterfish and yellowfin tuna.

You can also fly to Baja, and fish out of a resort, where accommodations usually include Spanish-style rooms, air conditioning (or room coolers), meals, cantina, open-air dining verandas (inside in winter, if weather is cool), swimming pool and, at the more posh establishments, tennis courts, horseback riding and cocktail bars in the swimming pool. Charter cruisers are available, along with rental fishing tackle.

Long-range fishing trips departing from San Diego, California, also sail down the Pacific side of Baja, to reach the big-game grounds. To reach the exotic species, you'll need to take at least an 8- to 10-day trip, and a 13- to 16-day long-range trip to the Revilla Gigedo islands will increase even more your chances of catching wahoo, dorado, and tuna.

Usually, long-range trips produce many more yellowfin tuna and wahoo than the number caught per angler out of a Baja resort, but catches of billfish on the long-range trips are usually only incidental, and roosterfish are exceedingly rare.

Many International Game Fish Association (IGFA) world-record catches have been made off Baja California. The 1980 edition of "World

Wahoo are one of the chief species taken on long-range trips to the Revilla Gigedo island chain, south and southwest of the tip of Baja California. This big wahoo weighed 90 pounds and was taken on a trolling lure.

Record Game Fishes," published by the IGFA, contains 24 line-class world records for six species caught in Baja waters: dorado (dolphinfish), 1; striped marlin, 4; roosterfish, 11 (out of 13 worldwide records); sailfish, 3; swordfish, 2; and yellowfin tuna, 3.

A partial listing of some of the most noteworthy world-record achievements follows:

DOLPHINFISH, 73 pounds 11 ounces, on 30-pound line, caught by Barbara Kibbee Jayne, July 12, 1962, off Cabo San Lucas, Baja California.

MARLIN, STRIPED, 250 pounds, on 12-pound line, caught by R. M. Anderson, April 16, 1965, off Palmilla, Baja California.

ROOSTERFISH, 114 pounds, on 30-pound line (also the all-tackle world-record), caught by Abe Sackheim, June 1, 1960, off La Paz, Baja California.

SAILFISH, 198 pounds, on 30-pound line, caught by Charles Kelly, August 23, 1957, off La Paz, Baja California.

BROADBILL SWORDFISH, 183 pounds 8 ounces, on 20-pound line, caught by Charles C. Yamamoto, May 4, 1971, off Cabo San Lucas, Baja California.

TUNA, YELLOWFIN, 388 pounds 12 ounces, on 80-pound line, caught by Curt Wiesenhutter, April 1, 1977, off San Benedicto Island, Baja California.

WHOPPER WAHOO TAKEN OFF BAJA

Most wahoo caught off Baja California aboard San Diego-based long-range boats weigh in the 35- to 60-pound class, although 70- and 80-pounders are not at all rare. A few wahoo exceeding 100 pounds have in recent years been taken aboard long-range boats, including a pair of giants landed in November, 1979.

Fishing aboard the *Royal Polaris*, out of Fisherman's Landing in San Diego, Scotty Castle of San Diego landed a 106½-pound wahoo that outweighed her by 7½ pounds. She caught the wahoo at the 23-Fathom Bank (see accompanying map), while casting a small Baby-X Salas lure on 40-pound test line. Miss Castle's catch fell 6½ pounds short of the current IGFA Women's World Record for that line class, a 113-pound wahoo caught in 1967 off Yanuca, Fiji, by Jan K. Kates.

An even larger wahoo — a 120-pounder — was hauled aboard the *Mascot VI*, from H & M Landing, by Joe Talosey of Bellflower, California, who hooked the fish at Thetis Bank (see map). Talosey was trolling a Salas TNT lure on 80-pound test line when the giant wahoo struck, and three gaffs were needed to hoist the wahoo aboard. Talosey's catch was 29 pounds less than the current all-tackle IGFA mark — a 149-pound wahoo caught in 1962 in the Bahamas by John Pirovano.

More recently, in February, 1980, Herbert Okada of Los Angeles, California, landed a 105-pound wahoo aboard the *Polaris Deluxe*, from Fisherman's Landing.

World-Record Yellowfin Catches Taken at the Revilla Gigedo Islands

Date	Angler/City	Weight	Location	Line Class
1-18-71	Gil Gardner, Firebaugh, CA (no longer current)	291-0	San Benedicto Is.	130*
3-7-71	Ed Malner, Garden Grove, CA (no longer current)	296-0	San Benedicto Is.	80*
1-18-73	Harold Tolson, Gardena, CA	308-0	San Benedicto Is.	130*
1-10-74	John Lightey, Torrance, CA (no longer current)	298-0	Socorro Is.	80
1-14-75	John Lightey, Torrance, CA (no longer current)	302-0	Socorro Is.	80
4-1-77	Curt Wiesenhutter, Long Beach, CA	388-12	San Benedicto Is.	80**
3-10-78	Joseph Semunovich, Gridley, CA	289-6	Clarion Is.	50

Source: International Game Fish Association Records
* Previous all-tackle records
** Current all-tackle records

TACKLE FOR TAMING BIG-GAME TROPHIES

Should Baja California suddenly crack along the U.S. border and fall off into the ocean, a healthy portion of the Southern California fishing tackle business would probably sink with it.

When a customer walks into a Southland shop and says the two magic words—"Baja" and "tackle"—the proprietor smiles, rubs his hands together and thinks it may not be such a bad day, after all. This not-so-small contribution to the local economy occurs because quality tackle is needed for Baja gamefishing, and well-outfitted tackle stores are virtually nonexistant south of the border.

Fishing tackle requirements for big-game fishing vary greatly, depending on an angler's skill, his sporting inclination and his pocketbook. What one person considers "light" tackle, another person might see as "medium" tackle; what one angler says is "ideal" gear for a particular species

may be judged too heavy or too light by a second fisherman. Many fishermen, for example, use 50- or 60-pound test lines for striped marlin fishing, yet striped marlin have been landed on as little as 6-pound test line—and not by accident, but by expert, light-tackle enthusiasts specifically fishing for marlin.

For these reasons, the following general Baja tackle recommendations should be taken as just that—*recommendations* and not as rigid requirements. You may prefer to use lighter, or heavier, or more, fishing tackle.

Generally, trolling for broadbill swordfish, blue marlin and black marlin, plus the giant-size yellowfin tuna, requires the use of heavy tackle. Lines testing from 50- to 130-pound test are used, spooled on big-game reels like the Penn International 50W, 80 or 80W which, in turn, are mounted on one-piece, heavy-action trolling rods with roller tips and roller guides (a nonroller rod would be used, with a similar heavy-action, for live bait fishing). For trolling, the rods should have a gimbal fitting on the rod butt, to match the gimbal cup on the boat's fighting chair. All aluminum rod butts are becoming more popular, because they are very strong, yet light weight.

Monofilament line may be used for trolling, but an angler has the advantage of less stretch in the line (an aid in setting the hook) when dacron line is used. Many long-range boat skippers, however, do not like (or do not allow) dacron line aboard when *teams* of trollers are trolling in the stern. The dacron is more prone to "wind toss" and, therefore, tends to be thrown around and tangle more with mono lines when a breeze is up, or when the boat makes a turn.

Striped marlin, wahoo, sailfish, dorado, smaller tuna and roosterfish are often taken on lighter tackle — 30- to 50-pound test lines, International 30 or 50 size reels and medium-action trolling rods or live bait rods. These same species are also grand sport on light tackle outfits, International Model 12 or 20 reels, 12- to 20-pound test lines and light-action rods.

Trolling lures most commonly used are vinyl-skirted types, the so-called psychedelic lures. Models like the Sevenstrand Clone, Boone Sundance Striker, Boone Jet-Scoop and Trainor Jig are good examples.

The larger vinyl lures, up to about 14 inches long, are trolled for the billfish and tuna, although these larger fish will sometimes strike a much smaller feather being towed for dorado, wahoo or lesser species.

Frozen flying fish are occasionally used as marlin trolling baits, although they have lost some of their angler appeal in recent years as the psyches have become more popular. (Ironically, a good portion of the Baja supply of flyers comes from Catalina Island, Southern California). When flying fish are used, they are trolled via the long outrigger poles and towed just fast enough to make them skip across the water.

Another trolling-lure type, used almost exclusively aboard long-range boats for giant tuna and wahoo, is the cast-metal jig, sporting a tail-treble hook and two, forward-riding trap hooks, added via short wire leaders, to increase the number of wahoo and tuna hookups. Examples: Salas ABC, TNT; Tady BCL; Rod Bender Dyn-A-trol; plus the 24-ounce Japanese-head trolling feathers sporting bullet-shaped, chrome head and black feathers. A variety of chrome-plated or pearl-headed "tuna-type" trolling feathers also work.

Generally, billfish trolling lures should have at least a 10- or 12-foot leader in front of them, the long leader helping to protect the main fishing line from a wildly jumping marlin or sailfish which may tail-kick the leader and wrap the leader around its bill during the fight. The leader, from 200- to 350-pound test, also protects the main line from abrading against the rough texture of the fish's bill. Some anglers prefer wire leader, which is not subject to fraying; the disadvantage to wire is that it can kink, or get wrapped in the main fishing line (while a billfish is jumping) and cut the monofilament of the main line. Some fishermen also believe that a heavy-monofilament leader produces more *strikes* than wire leader.

A wire leader should *always* be used when wahoo are abundant, since these fish have razor-honed teeth which can instantly snip through even very heavy monofilament. I like 49-strand wire, which is *not* covered with monofilament. Shiny snap-swivels must also be avoided between the leader and the main line, when wahoo are around; instead, use a flat-black finish snap-swivel. Wahoo will strike anything shiny in the water, including a silver snap-swivel, thereby relieving you of leader and lure.

Siwash-style hooks are good choices for live-bait fishing for the marlin and swordfish. Hook sizes normally range from 7/0 to 10/0. The Siwash has a long, slender point, a tubular shank and a short-sliced barb, all of which aid penetration in a billfish's tough mouth (exception: swordfish, which have a relatively soft mouth).

What's the most forgotten, yet vitally important piece of tackle for marlin fishing—indeed, for any type of fishing? Answer: a good sharpening stone (or small metal file). Dull hooks are a chief cause of missed strikes, especially from bony-mouthed creatures like marlin and wahoo. Lure and bait hook points should be checked often for sharpness and retouched as necessary.

Live-bait marlin leaders are often made from 125- to 175-pound test monofilament. Leaders to 6 or 8 feet long can be used for slow-trolling a bait around a finning, surface marlin; for *casting* live baits, the leader can be shortened to 3 or 4 feet.

When marlin are feeding on the surface their tails can often be spotted at great distances and the strategy calls for manuevering the boat to within casting distance, without spooking the marlin, and pitching a live bait—usually a *caballito*, grunt or mackerel—to the finning fish.

Most of the very large yellowfin tuna caught on long-range boats are taken while at anchor at proven tuna spots, although sometimes breezing tuna schools will be spotted while passengers are trolling for wahoo. A common routine aboard the long-range boats is to spend a few hours early in the morning at anchor and fishing for tuna, then trolling for wahoo for most of the day, before anchoring up again for tuna a few hours before sunset. The lateday tuna bites, or "sundowners," can produce some torrid action.

Some of the very largest tuna, including a few of the world records, have been hooked at night and brought to gaff in less than 10 minutes.

How are such incredibly short landing times possible?

Skippers and anglers I've interviewed think the tuna get confused and disoriented at night, stay on the surface, and reverse course to swim directly to the boat. A 200-pound daytime tuna could easily produce a two- or three-hour battle against heavy gear, yet the same size fish hooked at night might swim half-heartedly toward the waiting gaffs. These strange actors probably don't realize they're hooked, or even in danger, until they hit the deck of the boat. Then the deck shakes like an 8.5 tremor on the Richter scale.

Live Spanish or Pacific mackerel are excellent tuna baits. Other good bets include the mackerel-like *caballito* (little horse) caught off Cape San Lucas and the Mexican scad, caught at the Revilla Gigedos. A 6-pound bait, of course, is little more than a crumb to a hungry, 300-pound tuna.

What's the best live-bait terminal rigging for these giant tuna? Well, take your pick.

A few years ago, it was popular to tie the mono fishing line straight to the 9/0 hook. Problem: Some of the largest tuna, with more developed teeth, eventually sawed through the mono. Next step: try wire leader.

Fishermen began experimenting with short pieces of wire — usually less than 8 inches long — to protect the line from the big tuna's teeth. The tuna didn't seem to shun a bait dragging wire, hitting it about as well as straight mono. Problem: sharks also liked the wire and, once hooked, were practically impossible to cut off until landed. Next step: try extra-heavy mono leader.

The 150- to 250-pound test and 18- to 20-inch mono leader worked fairly well, although it had at least three disadvantages. Problems: it was much thicker than straight, main line, 80-pound mono, and therefore more highly visible; it was difficult to tie; and it still consisted of only one strand of mono, which a big tuna or an accidentally-hooked wahoo could cut through. Next step: Try the Bimini Twist.

The Bimini Twisters came up with the idea that two lines are better than one, teethwise. So the main fishing line, usually 60- or 80-pound test, was doubled, via the Bimini, and tied to the hook. The result is that there's relatively good protection against a tuna's teeth and line abrasion, but a shark will usually cut itself free in short order. Problem: most wahoo quickly cut through the double-leader, too.

This steady progression of leader ideas shows that long-rangers are actively experimenting. Probably in a couple of years, and with more testing, one of these rigs will establish itself as the most ideal and popular.

One thing is certain—if you don't pack your line extremely tight, you'll be in trouble when a big tuna strikes. Line too loosely wound on the spool will cut into itself as it stretches under the tremendous pressure of a running yellowfin. This stretching constricts the line between its own coils and makes it dig so deeply into the spool that it hangs up, refuses to come away, and then snaps.

Some of the huskier anglers, those athletes over 200 pounds and six feet tall, can stand up and handle a 9/0 or International 80 reel, but most of the guys prefer the lighter and easier handling International 50W model. Nearly 600 yards of tightly-packed mono will fill the latter. If you lose *that much* line, you probably didn't want to get involved much longer with *that* tuna, anyway.

Built literally into the side of a cliff at Cabo San Lucas, Baja, the Finisterra Hotel annually hosts thousands of American angler-tourists who travel south of the border to battle marlin, dorado, tuna, roosterfish and other Baja exotics.

Putting maximum pressure on a giant tuna is best done with a special rod—often custom built—which is short, moderately-tapered, stout-tipped and modified with an extra-long, 16- to 22-inch foregrip. The long foregrip allows the angler to put both hands in front of the reel, for extra-power leverage while pumping and lifting a huge tuna.

Although some long-range fishermen load up with as many as 20 or more rod and reel outfits for these extended expeditions, it's possible to feel very comfortable with far less. Ideally, a good set includes: a #50 or 6/0 reel with 60- or 80-pound test, for trolling and bait fishing; #50 or 6/0 reel with 50-pound test, for bait fishing; extra-wide (Newell-converted) 4/0 reel with 40- or 50-pound test for bait fishing; regular size 4/0 reel with 30-pound line for bait, or small jigs; narrow-spool 4/0 (Newell-conversion) with 40-pound test for jigging; and a #500 size reel and 20-pound line, for catching bait.

Wahoo, smaller yellowfin tuna, dorado and roosterfish are often taken on live bait pinned to a 6/0 or 9/0 size O'Shaugnessy-style hook. The hook can be tied directly to the main fishing line (except when fishing for wahoo, when a 12″, single-strand, 70- to 90-pound test wire leader should be used), or a heavier, short length of mono can serve as a shock leader.

The tuna, wahoo, dorado and roosterfish will also strike cast-and-retrieve jigs, like the Salas 6X, 6X Jr., Christy II, the Tady 44 and 14. I use a single 7/0 Siwash for the tail hook, instead of a treble.

The large single hook is more difficult for a wahoo to throw, because it offers less prying leverage as the fish shuts and grinds its jaws. And the Siwash style, with its relatively small diameter shank and its easily-honed needle point, affords excellent hook-setting in a wahoo's bony mouth.

A reel equivalent to the Penn #500, Daiwa 50H or Newell 338 is adequate for the small-to medium-size fish, but a 3/0 or 4/0 reel will handle larger fish taken on cast jigs. Lines for casting jigs usually range from 40- to 50-pound test. Rods, in the 6½- to 7½-foot range, should have medium-action tips capable of handling heavy metal jigs.

Additional pieces of fishing tackle might include: assortment of casting lures; rod butt belt; vest or kidney harness; longnose pliers; diagonal cutters; crying towel (for the big one that gets away); light spinning outfit; WD-40 lubricant; extra mono and wire leader material; soft-metal sleeves and crimping tool (for wire leader make-up), bait-catching rigs (small, multi-feathered-hook leaders) for catching mackerel and caballitos; extra bulk spools of line; cotton gloves; long-billed fishing cap; suntan lotion or sunscreen; sunglasses; camera and film.

Tackle store owners have to make a living, too.

For anglers who don't have their own fishing gear, rental rod, reel and line outfits are available for the long-range boat trips out of San Diego, and at the Baja resorts.

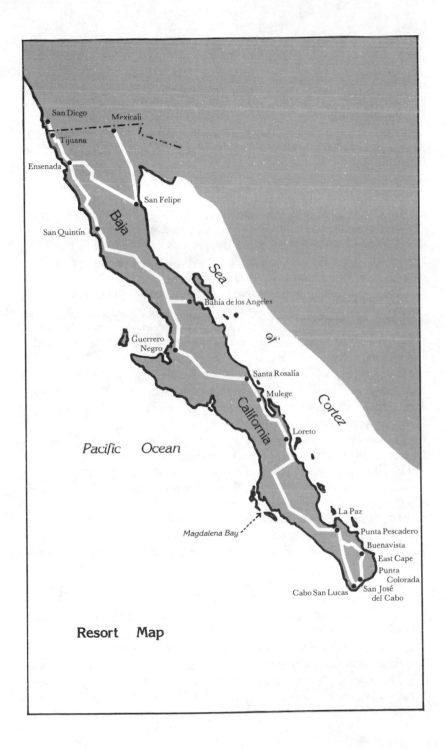

Resort   Map

HOW TO MAKE WAHOO HOLD ON

The wahoo is one of the chief species of big game fish caught during the wintertime long-range sportfishing season off Baja California.

Little wonder, with such relatively virgin wahoo grounds to fish as Socorro, San Benedicto, Roca Partida and Clarion islands, all comprising the Revilla Gigedo Island chain south/southwest of the extreme southern tip of Baja.

While getting wahoo to strike normally isn't a problem on these San Diego-based expeditions, getting them to hang on after striking can be difficult.

The wahoo strikes with such vengeance and velocity that it often hits in a blind rage, completely missing the hook, if not the entire lure. And frequently when they do connect, they will hit a lure amidships, latch on and then let go, unknowingly evading all barbs.

One veteran skipper once told me that if you land only *half* of the wahoo you hook, you're not performing too badly.

Evidence of the wahoo's wild attack is seen in the amount of fish which are foul-hooked—snagged in the head region or along the body—rather than cleanly stuck in the mouth.

Most of the wahoo hooked off Baja do not jump (infrequently some will make streaking leaps), but they will shake their heads violently under water, trying to rid themselves of a stinging aggravation they mistook for an easy meal.

To improve the number of wahoo landed, some long-range fishermen have turned to adding "trap" hooks to their trolling jigs (lures) in recent years. Such rigs do, of course, automatically disqualify any catch from being submitted for possible world record status, but most anglers fish for food, not fame.

Here's how to "trap" a trolling jig:

To rig the main leader, use a four-foot-long section of braided, 49-strand wire leader (Sevalon is an excellent choice) testing 130 pounds. Attach a large, *black* snap-swivel to one end by forming a loop with the leader material held securely by two soft lead sleeves crimped snugly in place. A black snap-swivel is used because wahoo will often strike any bright, shiny object (such as stainless steel swivels and snaps) and it can get extremely frustrating replacing entire trolling lure rigs after a wahoo has snipped off everything below the swivel. It can also get expensive.

Refer to the diagram to see how the metal sleeves are secured in place.

The other end of the leader is attached to the forward ring of the jig, again using metal sleeves to form a small loop in the leader running through the ring.

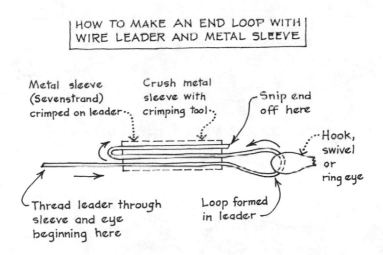

HOW TO MAKE AN END LOOP WITH
WIRE LEADER AND METAL SLEEVE

Metal sleeve (Sevenstrand) crimped on leader

Crush metal sleeve with crimping tool

Snip end off here

Hook, swivel or ring eye

Thread leader through sleeve and eye beginning here

Loop formed in leader

Now come the trap hooks.

The large wahoo jigs I prefer are about 14 inches long, so I cut two additional pieces of mono-covered wire which, after being attached to the jig, will make the trap hooks (size 8/0) ride about *half-way back* along the lure (see accompanying sketch). Attach one of the trap leaders to the underside of the jig by forming a loop through the forward lure ring; the other trap leader is attached similarly, but so that it rides along the topside of the jig.

Wahoo which whack the lure at mid-body, much like a dog grabs a bone, will discover an unpleasant surprise. Or if the lure slips out of its mouth, there are two additional hooks which may snag the fish.

Here are some other tips to make your wahoo hang on:

—Keep your hooks razor-sharp. Carry a small hone to touch up dull hooks. A properly sharpened hook should dig in when lightly pulled across your thumbnail.

—Set the hook hard *two or three times* immediately after a strike, but then *do not* try to reset the hook later. Hard sets at first will help ensure a solid hookup; resetting later can tear the hook out after the fight has worn a hole in the fish's mouth.

—Strive to keep any slack from occurring in the line, especially when the line signals that the wahoo is sulking and shaking its head.

—Don't pull a wahoo's head out of the water when it is alongside the boat ready to be gaffed. If you do, the fish could start thrashing wildly and throw or tear out the hooks.

Remember also to keep a cool head when a freshly hooked wahoo goes streaking across the surface, emptying your spool of most of its line and smoking your reel bearings. And that, perhaps, is the most difficult advice of all to follow.

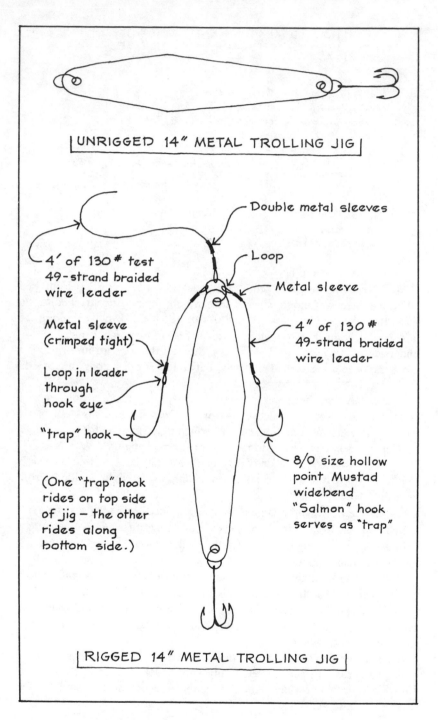

| UNRIGGED 14" METAL TROLLING JIG |

Double metal sleeves

4' of 130# test
49-strand braided
wire leader

Loop

Metal sleeve

Metal sleeve
(crimped tight)

4" of 130#
49-strand braided
wire leader

Loop in leader
through
hook eye

"trap" hook

(One "trap" hook
rides on top side
of jig — the other
rides along
bottom side.)

8/0 size hollow
point Mustad
widebend
"Salmon" hook
serves as "trap"

| RIGGED 14" METAL TROLLING JIG |

Fishermen troll for wahoo and yellowfin tuna aboard a long-range fishing boat underway in Baja waters. During the trips, anglers are divided into trolling teams and rotated so everyone has equal trolling time.

EXAMINING THE EXOTIC SPECIES

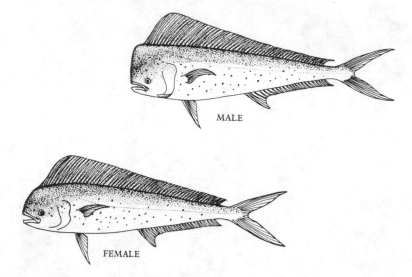

MALE

FEMALE

Dorado

Other Common Names: Dolphinfish, dolphin (commonly used, but incorrect, because it is confused with the mammal, dolphin), *English*; mahi-mahi, *Hawaiian*; lampugas, peje vapor, *Spanish*; shiira, *Japanese*.

Distribution: Worldwide in tropical and warm-temperate seas; prefers 72- to 88-degree water.

Features: Generally, the dorado is a rich iridescent blue or blue-green on the dorsal side; gold, bluish gold or silvery gold on the lower flanks; silvery white or yellow on the belly. Sides are splotched with spots ranging from black or blue to light gold. Body is long and sides thin. Very long dorsal fin with no protruding spines. Large males, sometimes called "bull" dolphin, have a high, vertical forehead, in contrast to the more rounded forehead of the females.

Angling Methods: Caught by trolling surface baits (flying fish, mullet, squid, strip baits, small bonito, caballitos, grunts) or artificial lures, such as small feathers, metal jigs or Rapala-type plugs. Also taken by casting live baits or chunks of bait. Often, the first-hooked dorado will bring the remainder of a school near the boat. The species likes to hang out around floating objects such as seaweed, logs, buoys.

All-Tackle World Record: 87 pounds, caught in Papagallo Gulf, Costa Rica, September 25, 1976, by Manuel Salazar.

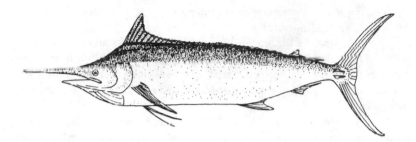

Marlin, Black

Other Common Names: white marlin, silver marlin, *English*; A'u, *Hawaiian*; marlin negro, aguja negra, picudo negro, *Spanish*.

Distribution: Tropical Indian and Pacific oceans. Species' distribution is sparser in open waters, more dense in coastal areas and near islands. Prefers 75- to 85-degree water.

Features: Quickest positive identification is through rigid pectoral fins that are set in a down position and cannot be folded flat against the body without breaking the joints. Sides of body much flatter than a similar-sized blue marlin. Dorsal surface of body is slate blue, changing to silver white below the fish's lateral line. Variations in color can produce a silvery haze over body.

Angling Methods: While black marlin can be taken on large trolling feathers and Kona-head type lures, a large, whole bait is often preferred, including mackerel, bonito, flying fish, even small tuna or dorado.

All-Tackle World Record: 1560 pounds, caught off Cabo Blanco, Peru, August 4, 1953, By Alfred C. Glassell, Jr.

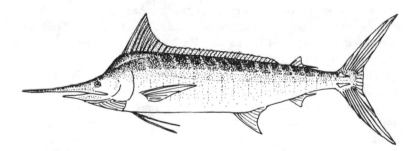

Marlin, Blue

Other Common Names: A'u, *Hawaiian*; kurokawa, *Japanese*; marlin azul, aguha azul, castero, *Spanish*.

Distribution: Found in tropical and warm-temperate seas, from 68- to 88-degree water temperatures.

Features: Back of fish cobalt-blue color, with flanks and belly a silvery white. Light blue or lavender stripes may appear vertically on body, but never as distinctly as in striped marlin. Pectoral fins never rigid, even after death. Fish has a slightly oval-shaped bill, heavy shoulders and broadly-forked tail.

Angling Methods: Taken by trolling large, whole baits—bonito, dorado, mullet, mackerel, caballitos, flying fish and squid. Also caught via large trolling feathers, or by casting large, live baits.

All-Tackle World Record: 1153 pounds (for Pacific Blue), caught off Ritidian Point, Guam, August 21, 1969, by Greg D. Perez.

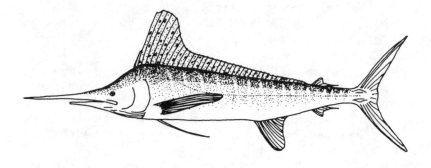

Marlin, Striped

Other Common Names: striper, red marlin, *English*; A'u, *Hawaiian*; maka, *Japanese*; marlin rayado, marlin listado, picudo rayado, *Spanish*.

Distribution: Found in Indian and Pacific oceans. Prefers 60- to 85-degree water temperatures.

Features: Steel-blue color on dorsal area, fading to bluish silver on upper flanks and white below lateral line. A number of iridescent blue spots found on fins; pale blue vertical stripes on sides of fish. Has high, pointed dorsal fin, which usually exceeds greatest body depth. Sides very compressed.

Angling Methods: Trolling with whole fish, feathers, Kona-head lures. Also caught on live baits while casting to surface-finning marlin.

All-Tackle World Record: 417 pounds 8 ounces, caught at Cavalli Islands, New Zealand, January 14, 1977, by Phillip Bryers.

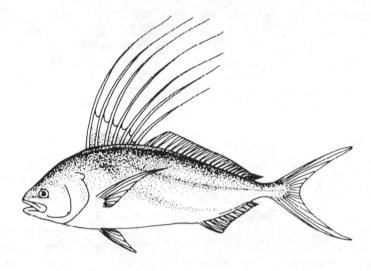

Roosterfish

Other Common Names: rooster, *English*; pez gallo, papgallo, *Spanish*.

Distribution: Found in the eastern Pacific, from Gulf of California south to Peru. Likes 68- to 85-degree water.

Features: A close relative of the jack family, the roosterfish is most distinguishable by its first dorsal fin, with seven long, wavy spines which resemble the comb of a rooster. The roosterfish varies in color, but often has a gray-blue, silvery-blue or black back, and a white or golden belly. Two dark, curved color bands run diagonally across the sides and toward the tail. Dorsal spines have dark and light stripes running horizontally across them.

Angling Methods: Trolling, mooching or casting small baits inshore, especially around sandy-rocky areas. Occasionally taken on cast-and-retrieve lures.

All-Tackle World Record: 114 pounds, caught off La Paz, Baja California, June 1, 1960, by Abe Sackheim.

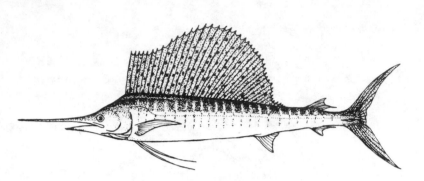

Sailfish

Other Common Names: spindlebeak, bayonetfish, sail, *English*; A'u lepe, *Hawaiian*; pez vela, aguja voladora, *Spanish*.

Distribution: Subtropical and tropical seas, usually near land masses, not in open ocean. Likes 72- to 85-degree water.

Features: Long, high, dorsal fin, with middle of dorsal higher than rest of fin; resembles a sail when fully raised. Back varies from steel-blue to black, changing to white or silver in belly. Dorsal sail is slate-blue, with black spots. May sometimes turn a deep-bronze color when brought aboard a boat, but bronze color does not remain after death.

Angling Methods: Taken by trolling strip baits, flying fish, mullet, feathers, plugs, saltwater flies. Also caught by casting live baits.

All-Tackle World Record: 221 pounds (Pacific sailfish), caught at Santa Cruz Island, Ecuador, February 12, 1947, by C. W. Steward.

Swordfish

Other Common Names: broadbill, broadbill swordfish, *English*; pez espada, emperador, *Spanish*.

Distribution: Found worldwide in tropical and temperate waters and along continental shelves. Prefers 55- to 70-degree water.

Features: Smooth, broad, flattened sword, usually longer than bill of other billfishes. A high, sickle-shaped dorsal fin. Adult swordfish lack scales. Color can vary on back from brown, bronze, purple, grayish-blue or black. Sides may be dark or light. Belly and lower sides musty white or light brown. Rarely travels in groups, but occasionally in pairs. Will occasionally attack boat hull with its spear, when hooked.

Angling Methods: Trolling baits on surface, or deep-drifting with live baits at night. In recent years, live bait casting with mackerel, bonito or caballitos has gained popularity.

All-Tackle World Record: 1182 pounds, caught off Iquique, Chile, on May 7, 1953, by L. Marron.

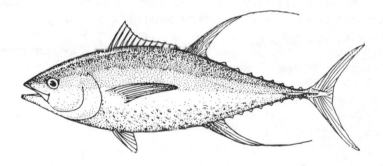

Tuna, Yellowfin

Other Common Names: Allison tuna, *English*; ahi, *Hawaiian*; atun de Allison, rabil, atun de aleta amarilla, *Spanish*.

Distribution: Found worldwide, in warm-temperate waters, in 60- to 80-degree water.

Features: Very long second dorsal and anal fins; may reach back halfway to base of tail in large specimens. Body football-shaped. One of the most colorful of all tunas, the yellowfin has a bluish-black back, lightening to silver on the lower flanks and belly. A yellowish-gold band (sometimes faint) runs from eye to tail. Fins are golden yellow; belly may have rows of whitish spots.

Angling Methods: Live-bait fishing with large mackerel, scads, caballitos. Trolling with large tuna feathers, marlin-type lures, strip baits, squid, flying fish.

All-Tackle World Record: 388 pounds 12 ounces, caught off San Benedicto Island, Baja California, April 1, 1977, by Curt Wiesenhutter.

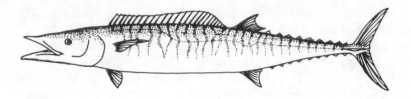

Wahoo

Other Common Names: oahu fish, Pacific kingfish, yahoo, *English*; ono, *Hawaiian*; peto, peto sierra, sierra wahoo, *Spanish*.

Distribution: Found worldwide, in warm-temperate and tropical seas, in 70- to 86-degree water.

Features: Body very long, with very long first dorsal fin that is about same height along its length. Snout sleek and pointed. Well-defined lateral line dips noticeably near middle of first dorsal fin. Color usually deep-blue on back, changing to silver on lower flanks and belly. Sides have several bright blue vertical bands. Mouth full of short, stubby, razor-honed teeth.

Angling Methods: Trolling with large feathers or cast-metal jigs; live-bait fishing with anchovies, mackerel, caballitos. Also hooked on cast-and-retrieve metal lures.

All-Tackle World Record: 149 pounds, taken off Cat Cay, Bahamas, June 15, 1962, by John Pirovano.

Fishing Areas, Seasons for Baja Big Game

Following is a brief rundown showing the best approximate fishing seasons and locations for various exotic species of Baja big-game fish. Information listed is intended only as a *guide*, since seasonal conditions such as water temperatures, water clarity, the influences of changing ocean currents and the availability of forage fish can alter traditional big-game fish migration patterns and numbers.

Marlin, Striped The striped marlin is taken, in at least some numbers, virtually year-around near the tip of Baja California, Cabo San Lucas. The species ranges north along the Pacific side of Baja, as far as Southern California, in the late summer and early fall, then migrates south to an area below Magdalena Bay (about 550 miles south of San Diego) for the winter. As water temperatures warm again in the spring and summer, striped marlin move north in the Sea of Cortez. A few are caught as far north as Loreto and Mulege, but they are not common there.

Generally, the best marlin fishing occurs south of La Paz, Baja California, off a stretch of coast extending roughly 150 miles to Cabo San Lucas. Good marlin fishing areas are found off Punta Pescadero, Buena Vista, Punta Colorada, San Jose del Cabo and Cabo San Lucas. Offshore from Cabo, the species is taken at the Jammie Banks, Golden Gate Banks, Lusitania Banks and the Gordo Banks.

Marlin, Blue or Black   These large-size marlin are primarily winter fish, hitting best (although in relatively small numbers) in November, December and January (some have been caught much later, as exceptions are often the rule in fishing). Most are taken from La Paz south to Cabo San Lucas. A few blue marlin have also been caught aboard long-range sportfishing boats from San Diego, fishing the Revilla Gigedo Islands.

Sailfish   Although the season varies, this species is usually found in greatest numbers from late May through August, off the lower Baja California peninsula.

Dorado   The dorado or dolphinfish appears to go through large cycles of relative abundance, sometimes being super-abundant one year, and conspicuous by their absence the next. Some dorado are caught in the lower portions of Baja practically year-around, but the largest concentrations often appear in winter and spring. Hold-over dorado hit well off Cabo San Lucas and the La Paz to San Jose del Cabo region during the summer, but big schools also migrate north into the upper reaches of the Sea of Cortez, as far as the Midriff Islands.

Tuna, Yellowfin   Depending on seasonal variations, this species may move as far north in the Sea of Cortez as the Midriff Islands, usually in late summer or early fall. On the Pacific side of Baja, yellowfin tuna can range as far up as the lower reaches of Southern California, when annual water temperatures reach their peak in the early fall. The best yellowfin tuna fishing is usually in the East Cape and Cape regions, from La Paz south to Cabo San Lucas.

In the winter, from late November through April, long-range boats from San Diego fish for 20- to nearly 400-pound yellowfin tuna at the Revilla Gigedo island chain, from 225 to 390 miles south and southwest of Cabo San Lucas.

Wahoo   The sleek-snouted wahoo is a southern-area swimmer, usually staying in the East Cape and Cabo San Lucas region of Baja, and venturing north along the Pacific side of the peninsula to Thetis Bank, off Magdalena Bay (about 550 miles south of San Diego), although a few schools may appear closer to the U.S., off Uncle Sam Banks.

Small, stray wahoo have been caught as far north as the Coronado Islands, 18 miles below San Diego, but these instances are rare. Wahoo are very abundant at the Revilla Gigedo island chain—Roca Partida, and Socorro, San Benedicto and Clarion islands.

Roosterfish This peculiar-looking species, with its long, wavy pectoral spines resembling the comb of a rooster, ranges some distance up the Pacific side of Baja from Cabo San Lucas, but just how far is unclear, due to the lack of resort-based boats fishing along the lower Pacific Coast side. Roosterfish are found in the inshore area of the lower Baja coast and into the Sea of Cortez, usually around sandy and rocky beaches, at Cabo San Lucas, San Jose del Cabo, Punta Colorada (one of the hot spots), Rancho Buena Vista, Punta Pescadero (an area north, at Punta Arena Norte, is excellent), Loreto and Mulege.

Catches to the north, off Loreto and Mulege, usually do not approach the numbers of roosters taken in the East Cape region.

A Pair of Baja Fish Tales

The One That Got Away . . .

There was a true fish tale born at Rancho Buena Vista Resort, between La Paz and Cabo San Lucas on the lower Baja peninsula, after a prolonged fight with a giant blue marlin of undetermined size.

Some years ago, five anglers in a Rancho Buena Vista charter boat hooked a behemoth blue marlin variously estimated at 1500 to 1800 pounds, by those who saw the fish. The blue, fighting doggedly from the second it was hooked, towed the boat and its contingent of fishermen several miles to sea, during an ordeal which lasted nearly 48 hours.

During the match, other resort boats had to ferry-out and transfer food, water and diesel fuel to the boat engaged in the marlin struggle and, once, even the *boat* was changed when mechanical problems developed.

Finally, after nearly two days, the marlin broke the line.

Take A Wahoo To Dinner . . .

The term "wild" is sometimes too-loosely used by writers in describing the behavior of game fish, but the word is definitely appropriate in detailing the behavior of a wahoo.

Wahoo, at times, will leap from the water *several yards* from a trolled feather or metal lure, then pounce down on the artificial as they crash back into the sea. Clocked in short bursts at up to 50 miles an hour, the fish produce sizzling runs which can quickly ruin a reel's drag mechanism; wahoo can swap ends so fast that they literally leave a fisherman standing in his tracks, while attempting to chase a hooked fish around the deck. They can stretch a line so taut that the monofilament or dacron will sing in the breeze.

Wahoo don't confine their wild antics to being hooked, either.

On a few occasions, in their haste to catch a fast-retrieved lure, unhooked wahoo have jumped clear of the water and landed aboard sportfishing boats.

In the mid-1970s, a 50-pound wahoo chasing a lure which an angler was lifting from the water decided it wanted the jig, anyway. The fisherman was aboard the long-range boat *Red Rooster*, out of San Diego, and so were four other persons who were sitting down to a quiet lunch of spaghetti in the vessel's galley.

The jig-chasing wahoo bounded over the handrail of the boat, barely missing the fisherman, crashing through a plexiglas, galley window and landed on the table in the middle of the spaghetti, quickly scattering the four passengers sitting there.

Later during the trip, the wahoo—filleted and deep-fried—was invited to dinner.

Regulations for Baja Travel and Fishing

If you cruise your boat south to Baja waters, in search of big-game fish there, or trailer a small craft down the Mexico 1 Highway, there are certain permits and licenses required by the Mexican government.

For small boaters, a trailer-boat license ($5 per month at this writing) is required, although enforcement at border crossings of this rule seems to be inconsistent. Still, it's certainly not worth chancing a citation, for the nominal cost involved. Trailer-boat licenses are available at all Mexican Consulate offices and at some San Diego area tackle shops which specialize in Mexico fishing. In the border area, a good source of such permits is Instant Mexican Auto Insurance, 223 Via de San Ysidro, San Ysidro, CA 91273 (714) 428-3583.

All trailer boats, trailers and vehicles should be covered with collision and liability insurance, by an underwriter recognized by the Mexican Government. This insurance, available on a per-day basis, may be obtained at various insurance agencies in the border areas or, by members, through the Automobile Club of Southern California.

Port-clearance papers must also be carried aboard any sea-going boat traveling to Baja, to be presented to the Port Captain at the first Mexican port of entry. Mexican Consulate offices issue such documents, as do authorized yacht-clearance services. An excellent source for clearance papers is Romero's Mexico Service, 1600 W. Coast Highway, Newport Beach, CA 92663 (714) 548-8931.

Tourist permits are necessary for traveling in the lower reaches of Baja California. These permits are available at Mexican consulates or, if you fly, through travel agencies or at Mexican airline service counters at major airports. They can also be obtained through the Automobile Club of

Southern California. There is no charge for the permits, but you must show proof of U.S. citizenship and carry such proof with you during your stay in Baja.

Fishing permits are also necessary, and may be purchased at Mexican Government Fish Commission offices, some San Diego area tackle stores, at Romero's Mexico Service and at Mexican insurance underwriters' offices near the border.

Mexican Government Fish Commission offices are located at 395 W. Sixth St., Room 3, San Pedro, CA 90731; and at 223 A St., Suite 709, San Diego, CA 92101; Regional offices of the Mexican Consulate are located at 601 W. Fifth St., Los Angeles, CA 90017; and at 1007 Fifth Ave., San Diego, CA 92101.

Tourist permits are not required individually aboard the long-range sportfishing boats departing from San Diego, as necessary clearances and U.S. Customs listings are provided by the boat operators. Cost and possession of Mexican fishing permits is also included in the long-range trip package.

Baja California Travelers' Tips

1. Take along plenty of U.S. coins and small bills, otherwise, during transactions, it's sometimes difficult obtaining exact change in U.S. currency.

2. Don't forget a good, sunburn-treatment aerosel spray, to soothe and heal you skin if you get overexposed. And take along suntan lotion, a sunscreening agent, sunglasses and a wide-brimmed hat.

3. Take *all* the fishing tackle you think you'll need, plus spare parts and extra line. Tackle supplies are often substandard south of the border.

4. Don't forget your camera, and film, and don't forget to use them.

5. Avoid the water in large cities (such as La Paz) if your system has a tendency to be affected by intestinal disorders (also called the *Turista* or *Montezuma's Revenge*). Resort water poses few problems, since it is pumped from deep wells.

6. Dress at most resorts and throughout Baja is informal.

7. Relax, unwind, and let yourself quickly grow accustomed to the friendly people and the slower-paced life.

Long-Range Info: Where to Write

Information regarding long-range sportfishing trips out of San Diego, California, to Baja big-game waters, may be obtained by contacting:

Palm's Long Range Sportfishers, Foot of Emerson Street, San Diego, CA 92106 (714) 224-3857.

Fisherman's Landing, 2838 Garrison Street, San Diego, CA 92106 (714) 222-0391.

H & M Landing, 2803 Emerson Street, San Diego, CA 92106 (714) 222-1144.

Point Loma Sportfishing, 1403 Scott Street, San Diego, CA 92106 (714) 223-1627.

Resort Information, Reservation Listing

For information about Baja's exotic gamefishing, or to make resort reservations or obtain rates for lodging and charter boat trips, contact the following sources. Most sources will send a free brochure, describing accommodations and costs, on request:

MULEGE

Hotel Serenidad, Mulege, Baja California Sur, Mexico, or P.O. Box 520, Corona, CA 91720 (714) 735-8223.

LORETO

Flying Sportsman Lodge, P.O. Box 17750, San Diego, CA 92117 (714) 270-2482.

Hotel Oasis, Loreto, Baja California Sur, Mexico.

LA PAZ

Hotel Los Arcos, Baja Hotel Reservations, 10941 Bloomfield Street, Suite F, Los Alamitos, CA 90720 (213) 594-4571.

PUNTA PESCADERO

Hotel Punta Pescadero, P.O. Box 1044, Los Altos, CA 94022, (714) 948-5505.

LOS BARRILES/BUENA VISTA

Hotel Palmas de Cortez, P.O. Box 1284, Canoga Park, CA 91403 (213) 883-2046.

Rancho Buena Vista Resort, P.O. Box 1486, Newport Beach, CA 92663 (714) 644-8838.

Hotel Playa Hermosa, P.O. Box 1284, Canoga Park, CA 91403 (213) 883-2046.

Hotel Club Spa Buena Vista, P.O. Box 2573, Winnetka, CA 91306 (213) 703-0930.

PUNTA COLORADA

Hotel Punta Colorada, P.O. Box 2573, Canoga Park, CA 91306 (213) 703-1002.

Laguna Guesthouse, 10406 Gaybrook Ave., Downey, CA 90241 (213) 869-8844.

SAN JOSE DEL CABO
Hotel Palmilla, P.O. Box 1775, La Jolla, CA 92037 (714) 454-0600.

CABO SAN LUCAS
Hotel Cabo San Lucas, P.O. Box 48088, Bicentennial Station, Los Angeles, CA 90048 (213) 655-4760.

Hotel Finisterra, Baja Hotel Reservations, 10941 Bloomfield Street, Suite F, Los Alamitos, CA 90720 (213) 594-4571.

Hacienda Hotel, P.O. Box 1775, La Jolla, CA 92307 (714) 454-1303.

Hyatt Baja at Cabo San Lucas, Apartado Postal 12, Cabo San Lucas, Baja California Sur, Mexico 1-800-228-9000.

Hotel Mar de Cortez, Apartado Postal 11, Cabo San Lucas, Baja California Sur, Mexico (telephone via local U.S. operator: Cabo San Lucas, 3-00-32).

Hotel Solmar, P.O. Box 383, Pacific Palisades, CA 90272 (213) 459-3336.

Twin Dolphins Hotel, 1730 W. Olympic Blvd., Suite 406, Los Angeles, CA 90015 (213) 386-3940.

A Final Word

I once wrote in a weekly saltwater column that there are three basic types of ocean fishermen: those who strive to catch the most fish of the group; those who must catch the largest to be ego enriched; and those with the maturity and wisdom to accept each fishing day as a chance to communicate with the sea, to experience the tang of salt air, the gentle roll of the boat, the graceful dipping of the gulls.

Unfortunately, some who are capable of catching the biggest and the most never learn a respect or a love for the resources of the ocean. And though their fish sacks may bulge, they return to port empty of experience.

After being hooked on a small trolling feather, a Baja dorado takes to the air off Loreto, in the Sea of Cortez.